The
BUSINESS
PLAYBOOK

The
BUSINESS
PLAYBOOK

Sports Strategies for Business Leaders

Brandon Steiner

CEO and Founder of STEINER SPORTS

with

Ken Shouler

and

Cary Steiner

Entrepreneur.
Press

Editorial Director: Jere L. Calmes
Cover Design: Beth Hansen-Winter
Composition and Production: Eliot House Productions

This publication is designed to provide accurate and authoritative information in regard to the subject matter covered. It is sold with the understanding that the publisher is not engaged in rendering legal, accounting, or other professional services. If legal advice or other expert assistance is required, the services of a competent professional person should be sought.

Library of Congress Cataloging-in-Publication Data

Steiner, Brandon.
    The business playbook: sports strategies for business leaders/by Brandon Steiner.
      p.   cm.
    ISBN 1-891984-96-9
      1. Business planning. 2. Strategic planning. 3. Success in business. 4. Sports—Psychological aspects. 5. Management. I. Title.
    HD30.28.S719 2003
    658.4'012—dc21   2003041950

Printed in Canada

09 08 07 06 05 04 03   10 9 8 7 6 5 4 3 2 1

TABLE OF CONTENTS

ACKNOWLEDGMENTS

J ared Weiss has been a great friend and partner. I was lucky to find a person who has so much in common with me. We have worked so hard together and had such fun for a long time.

Alzie Jackson at Camp Sussex in New Jersey was like a father to me. He showed me the way when the direction was far from obvious. He taught me and shared with me the lessons of life—good, bad, and ugly.

Matthew Lalin is a future star. He not only listened to me more than anyone but gave me the inspiration to write this book.

Thanks to Jere Calmes, Leanne Harvey, and Karen Billipp of Entrepreneur for their belief in and strong advice for this book.

A special thanks to Dale Adams for his patience and support.

I want to thank some key people at Omnicom Inc.: Michael Birkin, Tom Harrison, Bob Norsworthy, Greg Bedard, and Jason Cohen for all their support and business insight in helping make Steiner Sports bigger and better.

For my buddy "h," who showed me the importance of doing the right thing and taking care of people.

For Camp Sussex, a camp for disadvantaged children that pulled me out of Brooklyn for 16 summers and gave me a lot of love as a kid.

Thanks to great friends that I get to work and hang with every day—Larry, Cliff, Chris, and Nick.

A special thanks to all the kids I've coached in Little League. The 2001 Pirates, 2002 Diamondbacks, and 2003 Blue Jays won their championship in each of their respective years.

For all the people I worked for who believed in me—from the Hyatt Baltimore 1981; the Hard Rock Cafe grand opening staff, New York City, 1984; the Astor Group; and the Steiner Sports Staff of the last 14 years.

Thanks also to Phil Rizzuto and Mark Messier, who believed in me when no one else did.

Special thanks to Dan Klores and to the memory of Peter Seligman.

Thanks to Howard Rubenstein for taking an interest in Steiner when no one else would.

An author of several of his own books, Kenneth Shouler proposed this book and found a home for it at Entrepreneur Press. He interviewed many athletes, reorganized copy, and wrote the text.

My brother, Cary Steiner, was instrumental in generating an early version of the manuscript and arranging some ideas into chapters.

PREFACE

When I was a kid back in Brooklyn, the other guys and I would go to the schoolyard at P.S. 215 to play basketball. The schoolyard was a large concrete expanse with hoops all over. No full-court lines were drawn; in fact, I don't think any of the hoops even faced each other. We played half-court games, three-on-three when we had enough kids, or one-on-one when we didn't. No teams, no strategy sessions, no plans—we just played the game for fun. It was one of those times when not having a plan seemed to work out best.

I learned a few good shots—and after some hard knocks—a lot of rough defensive moves. The only time anyone calls a foul in a Brooklyn schoolyard is when significant blood flows. The rule remains: "no blood, no foul."

Two-hand-touch football was also an adventure, especially on city concrete. We strategized only one play ahead. We were just a bunch of boys trying to move the ball or defend a goal and having a good time banging into each other.

Looking back at those games now, they seem like the essence of unplanned activity: You showed up, picked teams, and played until you couldn't play any more. Who cared? It was fun then, and I will always think of it that way.

Later, playing Pee Wee football for the Kings Bay League and basketball at a Bensonhurst Jewish Community Center, I learned how important strategy and planning could be in sports. We always knew we wanted to win, but learning the steps that would take us to victory and deciding which strategies to employ made the games more exciting and more challenging. Sports became both a mental and physical exercise. Over time, I learned lessons that would serve me in business and in life.

Playing sports was step one in discovering a plan. As my life went on, I made plans then reworked them; made others and then refined them. I make my living in sports, but I've developed a business philosophy—a philosophy of planning a beginning, middle, and end to activities.

Since those old days on the playground, I've had conversations about planning with some of the greatest coaches and managers in sports: Joe Torre, Larry Brown, Bill Walsh, and Pat Riley to name just a few. Not one of them ever said to me, "We won by the seat of our pants," or "We winged it." Playing without a plan is all right for the Brooklyn asphalt, but it won't lead to the successful accomplishment of long-range goals.

I'm a "collector" of success philosophies. What I mean is, I talk to coaches, contractors, corporate CEOs, managers, manufacturers—you name them, and I've picked their brains and filed away their ideas about success. I also like to hear about the plans that athletes followed to become successful, just to see what I can learn. Why not? Athletes are good at what they do. We know them, or at least we think we do, because their feats are larger than life. Some people just look at the performances, but I see athletes themselves as unfolding stories—from childhood to college and from their professional careers well into their retirement. I like to trace the continuity and planning underneath the surface of the performances.

In this book, I want to share with you the principles that helped us build Steiner Sports from a $4,000 investment in the mid-1980s to a $35 million company. Steiner Sports is now a sports marketing and sports collectibles firm. But I was just a one-man shop when I started, with just a phone, a Rolodex, a corner desk, and high hopes for success. We now have 85 employees and are a bona fide leader in the sports marketing and collectibles industry. Our specialty is connecting athletes with corporate America. It's no secret that corporations want athletes for speeches, sports camps, and other public appearances and commercial endorsements. We make those connections happen.

We also expanded the business. Now it includes Steiner Sports Collectibles. We create licensed products, gifts, premiums, and signed sports collectibles. With the help of Steinersports.com, we now have more direct customers than could fit into Yankee Stadium—about 60,000 in all—and some 2,500 corporate customers and stores. Signing greats like the Rangers' Mark Messier and the New York Yankee shortstop Derek Jeter to exclusive autograph deals helped greatly in growing the business. Others in our stable of greats include Franco Harris, Jeremy Shockey, Chad Pennington, Sandy Koufax, soccer great Mia Hamm, Muhammad Ali, and Mark McGwire.

In 2000 we were acquired by Omnicom, a global marketing and advertising firm. We have a smooth working relationship. They own us, but we still maintain 100 percent our own identity. They open

Muhammad Ali autographing photos from his fighting days.

Photo courtesy: Getty Images.

doors for us; many of the chief officers in the Omnicom family help in showcasing our capabilities to top officers in the world.

No one is born knowing the principles that will lead to business success. I started out without a plan and without knowing the ideas that lead to greatness. I don't think that anyone who knew me when I was growing up thought I would be the head of my own company, certainly not a company as successful as Steiner Sports has become. No one would ever have imagined that I'd be the author of a book. I was perceived as a hard-working guy, a plodder who would make it through with hard work and persistence, but no one saw me as an "idea man." At John Dewy High School in Brooklyn I was the treasurer, and was involved with several clubs, like Future Business Leaders of America. But my combined SAT score in English and math was only 790, low enough that my guidance counselor suggested I should plan to go to a trade school rather than applying to college. As a graduate of Syracuse University, I'm glad I didn't listen!

Although college gave me an excellent education, I didn't learn my strategies of success there. Like many people, I needed to take stock of myself before I could improve my life and I needed someone to teach me what I didn't learn in school. In this book, you will see how I learned these strategies and how they can help you in any business venture.

You'll also read how these simple principles have helped great star athletes, many of whom I'm proud to call my friends and associates, reach their dreams and goals. In the chapters that follow, I offer various parts of the success plan that worked for me. I sincerely believe elements of the plan are universal, so others can profit from it, too. In large part, that is why I've written this book.

DEDICATION

I would like to dedicate this book to the person who has meant the most to me. It is for my wife, Mara, who loves me unconditionally, who is the only love I've ever had, and is the best partner anyone could ever have. Living with me, day in and day out, isn't easy.

It is also for my mom, who was really my mom and dad, and was way ahead of her time. She gave me the confidence and pushed me to make the changes I needed to be the person I am today.

Finally, it is for my two children who have given me more inspiration and love than one could ever ask for and whom I love more than anything.

Cal Ripken Jr. is named MVP at the 2001 All-Star Game in Seattle. Homering in his first at-bat at his final All-Star Game made him the standout, even though surrounded by all of baseball's best.

I look back at my career without any regrets. I sometimes say 'I wish that I would have not played so much,' but that's a banquet joke. But a lot of players look back over their career and they say, 'I wish that I would have played more. I wish I'd have taken care of myself better. I wish that I would have taken it more seriously.' I don't have any of those regrets.

—Cal Ripken, who played in a record 2,632 consecutive Major League Baseball games.

START WITH A ROAD MAP

I f you're planning a road trip, you'd be well advised to pack, get gas, and check your vehicle's oil and tire pressure. A map and a set of directions to your destination would also be nice. It's the same way on the road to success. You've got to know how to get where you're going. Some people call this knowing "the means to the end." You may not take every single road you've thought of, or stop at every sightseeing spot, but as Dallas Cowboys coach Bill Parcells says, "He who doesn't have a map gets lost." Parcells ought to know. He won Super Bowls XXI and XXV while coaching the New York Giants and later took the New England Patriots, a perennial doormat in the NFL, to Super Bowl XXX.

Our egos trip us up here. We don't like to stop and ask for directions (the joke is that men *never* do this); we don't like to look at the map. We like to believe that we know where we're going—but we usually don't know *exactly* where we're going. Why not? Because ego and pride says, "I'm OK. I've got this under control." But that kind of thinking leads to

Photo courtesy: Steiner Sports.

A Gatorade celebration over coach Bill Parcells. The photo was taken shortly after the New York Giants won the 1986 Super Bowl. Coincidentally, this is the first team to dump the Gatorade over a coach's head. It then became a tradition.

wasted time while we're spinning our wheels and driving around in circles. If you're lost on the road, sooner or later you've got to look at your map and get directions. If you're getting lost on the way to life's goals, you've got to do the same thing.

In his bestseller, *The 7 Habits of Highly Effective People*, Stephen Covey discusses the importance of "beginning with the end in mind." To Covey, beginning with the end in mind means, "knowing where you're going so that you can better understand where you are now and so that the steps you take are always in the right direction."

He thinks many of us fall into the "activity trap." We get waylaid in the "busy-ness" of life. The problem is people frequently stay busy without being terribly effective. Unless you know what is deeply important to you at the outset, and keep that picture in mind, you may end up achieving interim victories that are empty and come at the expense of more important things. Staying busy can be a kind of self-deception, keeping you from goals you deem truly important in business and life. The result is that people from all fields—lawyers and doctors, professors and business professionals—may awake one day, Rip Van Winkle–like, to find that their passionate drive to achieve blinded them to their true goals. In Covey's words, people often work tenaciously at climbing the ladder of success, only to discover "it's leaning against the wrong wall."

Success is a state of mind, and you always need to know what state you're in on your map.

CHOOSING YOUR DESTINATION

I walked into the office one morning after being out for a few days, and people in the office were telling me how great we were doing. I asked, "OK, let's go over things. What are the sales numbers?" The numbers weren't in yet. "How many calls have you made to your clients?—Did you make 50 a day? 75?" They weren't keeping track. "So," I asked, "how do we know we're doing great?"

Yes, good feelings are a definite part of success, but there's a lot more to it. You need a metric. You've got to measure your achievements against your goals to know where you are.

One of the challenges we face when setting goals is our ability to forget. That's why it's vitally important to write your goals down. Put them on paper and look at them every day. Being consistently aware of what you want and when you want it defeats your "built-in forgetter" and helps you stay motivated.

Everybody talks about goals and goal-setting, so let's define our terms. A goal must have three characteristics: (1) It must be specific. (2) It must have a date for completion. (3) It must be realistically achievable.

People say they want to make money and lose weight when what they mean is that they want to be rich and thin. Achieving these desires takes effort and planning—the stuff of goal-setting.

The more specific your goal, the better your chances of reaching it. Anyone can say they want to make a lot of money. But how much is a lot? If you don't have a specific amount, how will you know when you've reached your goal? It's easy to say, "I want to be better educated," but what exactly does that mean? Wouldn't it make more sense to say "I want to achieve a master's degree," or "I want to read a book a week for the next year?" Even back in the schoolyard we knew exactly where the basket was! Be as specific as you can with your goals.

Early in my business career, someone told me that a goal is just a dream with a date on it. For baseball Hall of Famer Gary Carter, the dream had a date. He wanted to make the major leagues by the time he was 21. Guess what? Like the people who built the Empire State Building, Gary got there ahead of time. He made it at 20 when he began playing for the Montreal Expos. From the late 1970s to the mid-1980s he was the best catcher in baseball and went on to hit 300 home runs, a feat accomplished by only four other Major League catchers—Yogi Berra, Johnny Bench, Carlton Fisk, and Mike Piazza.

A deadline makes your goal measurable by giving you a time frame in which to work. The best thing about this deadline is that it's self-imposed. If you miss your deadline, you can simply reset it, but having a date on your dream will help you work harder, faster, and smarter, getting you to where you want to be sooner and more directly.

PLANNING YOUR ROUTE

Having a plan—knowing where you're going, how you're going to get there—and then following the steps of the plan all contribute to the simplicity of achieving success. I may have begun learning these things on the basketball court and the football field, but making a plan and following it works everywhere for everyone, male or female, athlete or not.

Many of us walk through life, trudging through the day-to-day grind without a strategy. Later, we wonder why so many of our dreams remain unfulfilled. The purpose of this book is to help you formulate a simple game plan; a plan to become a champion in whatever field of endeavor you choose.

When Jim Abbott was asked how he pitched a no-hitter for the New York Yankees against Cleveland in 1993, he said, "I just tried to stick to the plan that I had going into the game." As a man who built a major league pitching career despite being born with only one hand, Jim Abbott knew the importance of a plan.

Of course you can live an unplanned life, being the ultimate free spirit and taking each moment as it comes. You can live in a whirl of spontaneity and have a lot of fun doing it. But true freedom comes with discipline, and without a defined goal or series of goals, without a strategy for reaching that goal and a set of tactics for implementing that strategy, you're running up and down the field without much hope of scoring any points. The tough news is that, while you may think you're playing two-hand touch, the chances of getting tackled are pretty high.

Your plans don't have to be complex. I once asked legendary basketball coach, Red Auerbach, about the "secrets" to the success of his great Boston Celtics teams in the 1950s and 1960s. Didn't the Celtics have something mysterious, some *je ne sais quoi*, like the formula for making Coca-Cola, which no other team knew? Red is an immigrant from Russia who grew

Photo courtesy: Getty Images.

Jim Abbott overcame his affliction and pitched ten years in the Major Leagues.

up in Brooklyn. He was brought up tough and is completely without pretense. He laughed in a kind of sneering way. "We had seven different plays on offense," he explained. "Bill Russell touched the ball on every one of them." Only seven different plays: I would call that effective simplicity. Nothing too complicated. The Celtics won every championship from 1959 through 1966, eight years in a row under Red, a record unmatched since.

I believe there are three kinds of people when it comes to success in life: The people who make things happen, the people who watch things happen, and the people who stand by and say, "What happened?" I want to help you stay in the first group. Making things happen is where the real fun is, and to make things happen, you're going to need a plan, and you're going to need to prepare.

MEASURING HOW FAR YOU'VE TRAVELED

People have tremendous misconceptions about success. What makes a successful day? Part of it is feeling good. Another part is having things going well in your personal life. But success in business means looking at your goals, your time lines, and seeing where you are relative to them. All business success is measurable, but many people don't take the opportunity to measure it often enough. Most people want to roll the dice for 30 days and hope they meet their forecasts. But that's not how a champion operates. In sports, you can't leave outcomes to a player's frame of mind or the winning or losing "streak" a team is on. A manager or coach is regularly looking at where his team needs to be and what it will take to get it there. In business, the reality is simple: If you want to do $1 million worth of business in a month, you've got to do $33,000 a day. That's $2,000 an hour. Success needs to be measured as often as possible because that's the map. Therefore, when you begin any project, have an idea of how you're going to measure your success. Plan to recap at specific points in your project so you can know if you're on the road to success or if you need to take a detour.

We all sell ideas, whether or not we sell products or services. We all make promises or guarantees to other people. We all persuade and convince. How can you really measure your success if you don't go back to the people you've convinced and make sure that your promise was kept? Part of measuring your success is making sure that you've fulfilled your word and delivered what was promised.

When he started out as a coach of the Los Angeles Lakers, Pat Riley had charts created of everything that happened in the game just played. *Everything.* Every shot, every rebound, every foul—even who gets possession of every loose ball!—they're on the chart. He creates charts for each player of current performance versus previous year, just like measurements reported by a corporation. This practice began in the early 1980s when Kareem Abdul-Jabbar requested that his coach come up with an objective measure for his claims about a player's hustle or lack of hustle. Riley complied with his center's request. With the help of assistant Bill Bertka, Riley created a measuring system called Career Best Effort. With this metric, players could see how they rated, not against each other, but against other players in the league at their position. In time, each player got to measure his present game against where he was before and where he wanted to go.

In less than a decade with the Lakers, Riley led his teams to five world championships. A mutual trust developed between him and Abdul-Jabbar. Abdul-Jabbar trusted in Riley's system of evaluation and Riley trusted in his Hall of Fame center with the unstoppable "sky hook" shot. In the crucial final minutes of games, Riley knew that Jabbar could get the team an important basket. "In the final seconds, teams knew we were going to Kareem," said Riley. "We went to him so often that it became an act of arrogance."

Obviously, athletes' achievements in their games are measured in many ways, but athletes also score outside of their playing fields, sometimes even after their careers have ended. Athletes naturally want endorsements and companies want popular athletes for their products. So companies refer to a marketing metric that assesses athletes' popularity. For athletes and other celebrities, the measure is called their SportsQ. Now you would think that by the time Michael Jordan has fully retired from the NBA, he would be tired of being measured for yet another statistical category. But this is just one more category he has dominated. Among sports personalities, Jordan still has the number-one Q score, with golfer Tiger Woods finishing second.

The company that compiles these ratings is Marketing Evaluations/TvQ in Manhasset, New York. Their scores are determined by surveys regularly mailed to a representative sample of 45,000 households that comprise their consumer panel. No one filling out a survey is paid more than the token $1 bill that marketing researchers have always used as an incentive. The panelists receive surveys with several hundred names, and they are asked to describe their familiarity with a personality ranging from "one of my favorites" to "poor" and finally "never seen or heard of." The Q Score is derived by dividing the total "favorite" responses by the responses from those who said they knew the personality. Put another way, Favorite ÷ Familiar = Q Score. The panel is also asked about favorite sports and products, so marketers can better link endorsers, products, and target audiences. Most every sports marketing or ad agency, not to mention TV and cable networks, purchases data from the company. Even celebs like Olympic gold medalist Mary Lou Retton and former New York City mayor Ed Koch call up to purchase their own Q Scores as they promote themselves for television and marketing deals. What's interesting is that Retton, who won the gold in gymnastics in 1984, and Koch, who was last New York City mayor in 1989, both are still being measured. We are always measured.

Measurement works in the corporate world, it works for coaches like Pat Riley, and it works for Steiner Sports. You'll do better with a road map, too. Our goals are always measurable, and I believe virtually any goal is achievable. I'm not the first poor kid from the streets of Brooklyn to become successful, and I won't be the last. I really believe that anyone can do just about anything. But some kinds of success—like building a business or writing a doctoral dissertation or a book—can appear pretty daunting, unless they're broken down into smaller goals.

KNOWING THE TURNS IN THE ROAD

There's a story about a boy who visited a wise old man and asked him for the secret of life.

The old man looked up and smiled at the boy. "The secret of life, my son, is knowing how to eat an elephant!"

The boy was puzzled and confused. "How, old man, can one eat an elephant?"

The old man laughed. "One bite at a time!"

The secret of achieving big goals is to make them bite-size. Let's say your goal is to make a million dollars. That's a specific amount. Now put a date on it. If you say, "I'm going to make a million dollars by next week," then in my opinion you're going against my third characteristic of goal-setting because in most cases, that's not realistically achievable. Now, if you set a goal to earn a million dollars in five years, that may be possible, depending on the skills, contacts, knowledge, and other resources you have or can get.

Breaking your goals down is like knowing the turns in the road. Knowing what your daily goals are, even your hourly goals sometimes, and measuring your performance against them will always let you know where you are and how near or far your goal is. Remember that you're not doing this measurement to discourage yourself! You're just keeping track, just learning whether you're on the right road, whether you're really on top of things or if you need some help.

On February 22, 1980, the USA Hockey Team defeated the USSR National Team by a score of 4 to 3 in the semifinal round in what some consider to be the greatest moment in the history of American sports. They went on to defeat Finland to earn the Gold Medal and overcome seemingly insurmountable odds.

Photo courtesy: Getty Images.

Linda Cohen is a sportscaster on ESPN's *Sports Center*. Her whole delivery is smooth and humorous. But it wasn't always that way. In 1994, she remembered being called on the carpet:

Here I am at barely the start of my glory—it was the New York Rangers' playoff run and the year they won the cup, the first time in 54 years!—and my bosses called me in the office and they say, "You know what? There are some things that we think you should be doing better. We know you know your sports and we're only going to give you another year, instead of the two years on your contract, to basically see if you can come through with what we think you can come through with."

So I came out of that office sobbing, just sobbing. Obviously, here I think everything is going wonderfully and it's not. And then I got motivated. When we face disappointment and rejection, we have that down time, and then that passes, and some people remain down and others are motivated by it. I basically tried to get specific with my bosses to find out what exactly did they mean. I became more like myself, which means not being worried about fitting somebody's view of a woman sportscaster. I became Linda Cohen, the person I am when the camera goes away and the mike is off, which is like Linda talking sports to her best buddy, OK? I was very conversational and let the real Linda come out, show off the knowledge, mix it, and do all that with personality.

I watched the tapes and saw that I controlled and kept that inside, now I found ways to bring that out without suffocating the viewer. And it was about finding a fine line that all sportscasters look for, and within the few months, six months I would say, it was all coming together. So it was like screech, halt on the brakes, look what you're doing, and stop trying to be something else, and just be myself. I was motivated by their criticism and thought, "I will prove you wrong." Within a few months they came to me and said, "Wow, you're doing everything we thought," and they extended the deal, and there were no issues. But they made me feel like a lame duck for a while, and I had to deal with that.

Linda's story shows that you may have to reassess your performance and make the necessary adjustments. Another point to remember when setting a goal is that there are circumstances beyond your control that can delay you. But they shouldn't stop you. Watching Linda over the years has been a real pleasure.

REARRANGING YOUR TRIP

It's also been my pleasure to know Earl Monroe. He was known as "Earl the Pearl" for his incredible spin moves and feints that kept every NBA defender off balance. Earl is a no-brainer Hall of Famer. For those of you who missed him in the late 1960s and 1970s, let me tell you that there was never any question that he would be elected to the Hall. He was simply one of the greatest guards ever to shimmy.

Earl Monroe came into the NBA in 1967 with a specific plan. He wanted to score 20,000 points. The 20,000 number is not arbitrary for a shooter. For a basketball player it means 25 points a game, 80 games a year, for 10 years. For Monroe it seemed to be a realizable goal, because he had averaged an other

Photo courtesy of: Getty Images.
Earl Monroe, a trailblazing and legendary NBA guard.

worldly 41.5 points a game in his last season at Winston-Salem State in North Carolina and became the most potent scorer for the Baltimore Bullets in the early 1970s. I asked Earl about that goal and he told me:

> If I had stayed in Baltimore, I probably would have done that. I played 13 years and didn't reach 20,000. When I came out of college my senior year, I knew I could score points. I know that the average tenure for a player is about four years, but I thought that ten years was about the norm for guys who started and played.

But before the 1972 season, Earl was traded to the New York Knicks. The Knicks had been a perennial NBA power since 1969. They relied less on individual stars and more on the team play of guys like Walt Frazier, Willis Reed, and Dave DeBusschere. The Knicks passed the ball so much that even Gene Hackman from *Hoosiers* would have been happy. That hadn't been the case in Baltimore, where Earl was a one-on-one guy and the Bullet's greatest offensive weapon by a wide margin. Earl's 20,000-point plan had to be changed, and he knew it.

> When I came to New York, I knew what was going to be happening with my career. I figured the 10-and-20 goal was not going to happen. I'd have to switch gears, so to speak, and think about other things. I thought about a championship. If you play the game, that's the ultimate you can achieve. The only thing that I basically did was take a back seat instead of a front seat. In Baltimore I had the opportunity to have a team that was essentially my team. In New York, I came to a team already established, and they had their place already; it was a matter of understanding what that was, and what the protocol was. I tried to fit into that scenario. Other things started creeping into my thought pattern—the most important of them was

becoming a student of the game. That was basically what I tried to do after I got traded.

He could still be "Earl the Pearl" if the Knicks needed him to go off on a spurt. On many nights he could still electrify the crowd. But he sublimated his personal goals and focused his efforts on making the team better. A year after he came to New York he was part of the Knicks' second World Championship. Monroe had modified his plan and still arrived at success.

Monroe understood that success involves planning. Most of us already know that. He understood more. He knew that success could be achieved in resetting his previous goals and making new plans to achieve those new goals. Not reaching his new goal didn't hurt his legacy. He was selected as one of the NBA's top 50 all-time players and voted onto the NBA's 50th anniversary team in 1996.

Several years back, my firm threw a dinner for our top clients and set up a 1973 Knicks reunion with him and all his teammates. It went so well; there was—and still is—incredible nostalgia for that team. There ought to be, too: The Knicks haven't won a championship in the 30 seasons since.

As Earl Monroe illustrated, sometimes goals have to be postponed or even changed, but with a solid goal in mind, I believe you can accomplish anything.

FACING DETOURS IN THE ROAD

You can also fit unexpected delays into your goal-setting. Remember Scotty from the original *Star Trek* series? Captain Kirk would ask Scotty how long it would take to do something, and Scotty would say, for example, that it would take at least 12 hours. "We need it in one hour," the captain would say. Scotty would answer, "I'll do what I can, Captain!" And it would always be done. But Scotty always figured "delay time" into his plan.

When it comes to writing a book, John McCollister, who runs The American Writing Institute, says, "Estimate what your time will be and then add half of that." So if you think a book will take 12 months, add six to get a more realistic time line for your goal. Then ask the publisher to allow you 18 months. Why? Reality intrudes on even the best-laid plans. You may have to take on other me-first projects you didn't plan on. Illness may beset you. Unexpected personal problems may arise.

They sure did in the case of Monty Stratton. Stratton was a Chicago White Sox pitcher from 1934 to 1938. In 1937 he was an All-Star pitcher. In 1937 and 1938 combined, he won 30 games and lost 14. But he lost his leg in November 1938 after accidentally shooting himself with a revolver while hunting rabbits.

Stratton worked to make a comeback, and in 1946, at the age of 34, "Gander,"—his nickname came from his 6-foot-5-inch, 180-pound frame—signed a contract with a Class C Texas team and won 18 games and lost 8. He didn't come back in a week, a month, or even a year; but Stratton set a goal to pitch professionally again, and he achieved that goal. No matter what gets in your way, a clear, well-thought-out goal can help you overcome any obstacle.

In 1949 the story of the gutsy pitcher's life was made into a movie, *The Stratton Story,* starring Jimmy Stewart. The subject matter must have inspired the writer, too: The film won the Academy Award for best original screenplay for screenwriter Douglas Morrow.

SEEING YOUR PATH

To be a champion, you need to empower yourself, and I mean that literally. I'm not talking about swallowing ten cups of coffee. I mean mentally and spiritually. Power your day! Use your imagination to visualize the things you want to accomplish that day. See yourself successfully accomplishing them. Loosen up and talk to yourself! I do it all the time. Talking to yourself doesn't mean you're crazy—it means you're thinking, imagining, and listening to your own thoughts. Talking to yourself

SCORING A DREAM

I had a goal in the summer of 1999. I don't expect many people in the world to have the same goal, but I sure took it seriously. For my 40th birthday, my wife, Mara, got me a ticket to play in Michael Jordan's Fantasy Basketball Camp at the Bally's Hotel in Las Vegas. The camp is for people 35 and older, and you meet other basketball crazy guys and get to play four-on-four games with Michael Jordan. Jordan brought along Duke University Coach Mike Krzyzewski; also from Duke, Dean Smith, Jordan's coach from the University of North Carolina; and Larry Brown, currently the coach of the Philadelphia 76ers. I was so psyched up to play in this camp, but I blew out my calf and had to go home. I was laid up for two months with the injury. To say the injury was upsetting would be an understatement.

The fortunate catch was that people who were injured could come back and play the next year for free. I spent the whole year getting in shape. I played basketball, ran stairs, and spent more hours than I care to remember performing aerobics.

Besides all the physical preparation, I visualized what it would be like to win a game against Michael Jordan, and I can tell you I got pretty motivated. I knew I would have a story to tell forever. I went back to the camp in the summer of 2000, and said to Jordan, "I had a dream: I'm playing against your team, and I'm gonna hit the game-winning shot in your face." Michael looked at me like I was nuts and said, "That's not a dream; that's called a nightmare."

The night before we played, I saw Jordan in the hotel, and I was still talking trash.

"Why don't you come down to the gym at 8 A.M.?" he asked.

"Make it 7:30," I said, "and leave those sissy powder-blue NC shorts at home."

The next morning we started a four-on-four game up to seven points. I was guarding Michael Jordan, and right away, he hits two shots from the perimeter. I want to tell you, those shots were just inside the three-point line, and he drilled them like they were free throws. He might have been retired for two years, but he could have played NBA ball right then and there. He was loose; I was in a deep trance. It's already two to nothing, and he looks at me and says, "You're done." I felt like former Knicks guard John Starks did. After Jordan, then 35 years old, scored on Starks several times in a row in Madison Square Garden in 1998, Jordan looked at Earl Monroe sitting courtside and shouted, "He can't guard me." Earl was so inspired watching Michael, no doubt remembering his own one-on-one exploits, that he got up and shook his fist as if to say, "Man, that's the way to do it."

Then Jordan let me take a shot, and I hit it.

"That was lucky," he said.

"If you were playing D, that wouldn't happen," I fired back.

My next time, I had what I thought was an open jumper. Jordan blocked the ball clean, swatting it so far that it bounced and rolled across the gym, three courts away. People say that when Celtic great Bill Russell blocked shots he managed to keep the ball inbounds so Bob Cousy or another teammate could grab it and start a fast break for Boston. Jordan had no such intention: That shot was blocked with such force that if we had been playing outdoors, it would have rolled off the lot, into the desert, all the way to California. My teammates knew that in my mind this had become a one-on-one between Jordan and me, and they told me to calm down.

Late in the game, Jordan was holding the ball on the perimeter, with his team ahead 6 to 5, needing a single point to win. He had an open shot, but the idea was to get others involved, so he passed up the shot and tossed the ball to a teammate underneath the basket. The guy blew a layup. It was our ball, and I got open at the top of the key and hit a shot. Jordan plowed into me and knocked me over.

"And you hacked me," I told him.

His team missed another shot. Now I wanted the ball back. It came to me, and I passed it to another guy. Then a teammate set a screen for me. Jordan could have broken through the screen, but one of his teammates got in his way. Suddenly, the basket seemed to open up and looked like a big, blue ocean. I threw up the ball, and it swished from 20 feet out.

"Sit the ##@&#*#@ down and watch me play," I yelled at Jordan.

Now there were high-fives and commotion all around, and Jordan's team had to sit down. I had a story I could tell for a very long time.

Photo courtesy: Larry Davis.

gives you the chance to rehearse your success, to imagine out loud how you'll handle conversations, speeches, and answers to questions.

Give yourself 15 minutes of creative visualization. Mornings are best; you'd get up 15 minutes earlier a day to increase your income, wouldn't you? So do it! This is about improving every area of your life. You can do it anywhere: on a train, lying in bed (although I wouldn't do it while driving a car!). Now, picture your goal. Picture yourself in possession of your goal. Imagine that you already have what you want, whether it's a particular job, making a big sale, cashing a huge check, or weighing yourself with a thinner body. No matter what your dream is, see it, touch it, taste it for 15 minutes every day.

In addition to energizing and empowering you, creative visualization also conditions the subconscious mind to start working in the direction of your goal. Visualization is powerful!

Of course, this assumes that you have a clearly set goal in mind. A champion always has a specific goal. I've never met a football player who didn't know which direction he needed to move the ball or how many yards to the end zone. Knowing what you want and what it takes to get there is key.

I can't say it enough—the journey of success is a lot smoother and more pleasurable when you know the goal to be achieved and how to get there!

—— *Chapter Review* ——

▶ Always have a road map. Know where you are and where you're going on the road to success.

▶ Write down your goals—don't let your "built-in forgetter" take control.

▶ Make sure your goals are specific, include a deadline, and are realistic.

▶ Keep your goals "bite-size."

▶ Don't stop—even if your goals are delayed.

▶ Are the goals you set truly your goals?

From left to right: Ozzie Smith, Derek Jeter, and Roy White conducting a clinic for Steiner corporate client's kids.

*T*he best advice in developing your career? Two things: One, find your passion because without it I don't think you can really be very good at anything you decide to do in life. And in addition to passion and finding what you really love to do, try to work and find the best people in the organization to have as your mentors and be totally open to their coaching advice. As a sponge, absorb everything you can.

—Tom Watson, vice chairman/chief growth officer at Omnicom.

FIND YOUR NICHE

For me, there's no thrill like the thrill of creating. I imagine it's the same for all of us—to see something we built where nothing existed before is the ultimate excitement.

To help you understand how my philosophy about success evolved, it might help for you to know more about our business. As I said, Steiner Sports is a sports marketing and collectibles firm with about 80 employees. But that doesn't begin to capture it. Think of it this way—we're a company composed of seven parts.

We manage other company's sports marketing activities, like athlete appearances, golf tournaments, commercials, press conferences to introduce new products. Companies hire us to find athletes.

So let's say Dannon Yogurt needs an athlete for its "winning moments" campaign. What we did was pitch Alcone, their marketing agency, on "America's Greatest Sports Moments," which included moments in sports with which most people would be familiar. We pitched them many other ideas, but they liked the "greatest moments" campaign best. So Dannon and Alcone visited us, just to see for themselves if we could handle a promotion that would be national in scope. We offered several names for spokesperson and they liked Mia Hamm best because her popularity and Q rating was appropriate for their customers. We then contacted Mia and signed her to a deal. Dannon ended up using a likeness of Mia Hamm on all their carton lids, and she was a representative of America's winning moments as a great soccer player. Customers could win prizes, like "Great Moments Collectibles," signed by players, depending on what was under the lid. Mia did a sales kickoff to announce the program, and became a spokesperson for Dannon in print, radio, and TV commercials.

We also coordinate athlete appearances with trade shows or private signings for a few hours. We might arrange for Cal Ripken to make an appearance at a VIP cocktail party or sign a few autographs at the trade show to attract traffic to a company's booth.

We also sell memorabilia wholesale, both to elegant stores like Bloomingdale's and Neiman Marcus, and to independent retail shops that resell our goods. That's the third part of the business. We also sell to mass-market stores like Wal-Mart, Target, and Kmart.

Steiner Sports brokers licensing deals where companies call us up and say, "We want to use Derek Jeter's image on this figurine. Could you get us his approval to do that?" So, we'll contact Jeter's agent Casey Close and make that deal. We have helped market Derek Jeter for collectibles, autographs, baseball clinics, and some licensing deals since 1996. He is in our offices about once a month, and we especially did a lot of business with him after he won the All-Star MVP and World Series MVP in 2000.

We're now in the fantasy business, too, where we create fantasy packages for fans. Someone might get two tickets to a game at Yankee

Stadium and get to meet Jeter after the game, or they could go to a New York Rangers hockey game, meet Mark Messier, and get an autographed stick and jersey. In addition, we have an event company that can produce a golf tournament with athletes or produce an event like the 2001 auction on the *Intrepid,* the aircraft carrier docked in New York, to benefit the families of victims from the World Trade Center attacks. On top of that, we ship some 100,000 memorabilia orders a year from Steiner Sports.

As I said, we built Steiner Sports from a desk, a phone, and a card file into a multimillion-dollar business that, with all of its separate parts, can still be boiled down to two companies: Steiner Sports Memorabilia and Steiner Sports Marketing.

There's been a lot of interest in sports marketing in recent years, starting even before the film *Jerry Maguire* came out or the edgy TV series *Arliss* became popular. Still, there's not a lot of understanding about what sports marketers are or what we do. Most people think that sports marketing is exciting and glamorous. It sometimes is. Most people think that it's a cutthroat business. It can be. Most people think that everyone in sports marketing represents athletes. Not everyone.

In the world of sports marketing, a lot of money is made creating relationships between corporations and athletes. These relationships can be long-term, such as when an athlete becomes a spokesperson for a company; or short-term, as with a celebrity endorsing a product or a company, hiring an athlete to speak at a sales meeting or other corporate event.

DO THE OPPOSITE

At Steiner Sports, the greatest share of our business comes from representing the corporate side, which is not the norm in our industry. Sometimes you have to see what most people are doing and *do the opposite.*

My first step in the "opposite" direction took place around 1987. I was at my friend Kevin Heller's wedding talking with Marty Blackman, a great sports marketer and one of the very few people who was matching athletes with companies at that time. He continues to be one of the true gurus of the business. I asked him, "How can I get into this business, Marty? I mean, I'm in it, but how can I get *into* it?"

"Well, Brandon," he said, "you've got two ways you can go: You can do what all the other people are doing, chasing after individual athletes and waiting for the phone to ring, or you can come up with some ideas and go to the companies and pitch *them* instead. They're the ones who have the money!" I could hear bells and whistles in the distance.

Marty went on to explain that once you have a commitment from a corporation, you can always find the talent. In fact, the talent will find *you*. It's the idea that counts. He told me that I'd be more likely to get a meeting with a corporate decision-maker than with an athlete. Of course, this idea meant I'd have to take the time to become a keener judge of talent, but that task would be balanced by developing more knowledge.

Of course, I didn't listen at first. I went after the athletes. I represented Darryl Strawberry, Keith Hernandez, and a bunch of other New York Mets in the late 1980s. I felt like my entire life consisted of either running in circles or sitting and waiting for the phone to ring, trying to put a deal together.

Photo courtesy: Getty Images.

When the Mets won their second World Series Championship in 1986, Keith Hernandez, a human vaccuum at first base, and Gary Carter were leaders.

At some point I got frustrated and started taking Marty's advice, getting meetings with corporate people, just tossing my ideas to them. I think the first real bite was a series of athlete-hosted boxing events with closed-circuit TV. We'd rent a restaurant or club with closed-circuit access to a big boxing match and book an athlete to host the evening. The corporate guests would look forward to watching the fight and sharing the experience with an athlete.

That kind of event grew into others: arranging and planning corporate golf tournaments with guest athlete players; creating some baseball and basketball clinics for kids; they were small things, but they were adding up. I thought then that I had found a new and promising direction. Looking back, because I had heeded Marty Blackman's advice, I had found my niche.

One part of finding your niche may be to travel in a new and daring direction.

DO SOMETHING NO ONE ELSE HAS DONE

This doesn't have to be a big thing. It can be something small, or a series of small things. Look around you. Something's not being done!

I once spent a summer selling knishes and cold drinks on the beach in Coney Island. I got paid by the knish. I was doing well, but since there are only so many ways to yell, "Get your knishes!" I needed something more. Because the little kids didn't like knishes as much as the older people did, I started carrying small packages of cookies with me, shouting, "Hot knishes! Oreo® cookies!" My sales zoomed upward.

As I said before, one way to find something new is to look at what's being done now *and do the opposite.* Let's face it, once I listened to Marty Blackman's advice, there was less competition—because no one else was doing what we were doing! We had a wider choice of athletes than with an agent. Not to mention, we could create fair deals for everyone concerned: the athlete and the corporation.

FIND YOUR PASSION

I asked Tom Watson of Omnicom (not the professional golfer)—the company that acquired Steiner Sports in 2000—what advice he would give a person trying to develop his or her career. His advice was so good that I began this chapter with it. I want to repeat it here so I can analyze it further.

"Two things," he said without hesitating."One, find your passion because without it I don't think you can really be very good at anything you decide to do in life. And in addition to passion and finding what you really love to do, try to work and find the best people in the organization to have as your mentors and be totally open to coaching advice. As a sponge, absorb everything you can and carry a da Vincian journal."

Here I paused. A da Vincian journal? Say what? He explained the journal was named after Leonardo da Vinci, the Renaissance artistic and scientific genius from Vinci, a hill village in Tuscany. Much of the originality of da Vinci's intellect was expressed in the notebooks he kept."In this journal you record all your thoughts and impressions and what you've learned from great people," Watson continued."It's a hard cover book that you carry around with you and record observations, thoughts, comments, lessons. I carried one all my life in spite of the fact that I use a computer.

"I would record in it lessons that I've learned on assignments, engagements that I've been involved with, things I want to remember, things that people have said that I thought were really insightful, sayings or aphorisms that might have gotten my attention, such as 'Optimism is true moral courage,' or 'Progress, not perfection, is what I'm striving for'—those types of things."

It wasn't exactly self-promotion that Tom Watson was after, but he was certainly after self-development, and the thoughts of great people can't help but inspire us.

But let's say you've expended all your creative energy and can't come up with anything new. Take a pad and pencil and talk to your coworkers and the people who report to you and ask them what they think needs to get done. Ask them what things could be done to help them move ahead. Believe me, you'll get a list! If you make that list a priority and start getting those things done, you'll be well on your way.

Know what you want to accomplish, and make sure you measure your results. Be able to show what needs to be done, what you did, how you did it, and the effect that your efforts had on your business, your relationships, and the people and things around you.

A champion becomes a champion for a reason, and the first step in becoming a champion is to know your reason, your "why."

Mia Hamm is one the world's greatest female soccer players; in fact, she's the first-ever three-time U.S. Soccer athlete of the year, male or female. With Mia leading the way, the University of North Carolina won four consecutive NCAA titles. Mia has played on co-ed teams as well as women's teams. She told me, "Personally, what I want to know is that I *matter*, that I make a difference, that this team, in order to succeed, needs me to be a part of it and then I need to know what that part is. I'll give everything I have to give if I know that it's of some importance." As a team player, Hamm will play a part, will fill a niche, but she wants to know what it is.

STAY POSITIVE AND KEEP POSITIVE PEOPLE AROUND YOU

When I asked New York Yankees manager Joe Torre what success means to him, he told me that the key for him is to focus on the things he can control and not worry about the things he can't control. For a manager, that means not worrying about injuries, bad calls by umpires, and other parts of the game that are a constant source of irritation. Instead, attention is focused on successful strategy and knowing players' tendencies

Photo courtesy: Getty Images.

Yankee players lift manager Joe Torre onto their shoulders and carry him off the field after winning the 2000 World Series.

well enough to put them in situations where they have the best chance for success. That's positive thinking.

Joe also said that creating a team means putting together a group of individuals who care as much about the people around them as they do about themselves, people who will work toward a common goal. Before the 1999 World Series against the Atlanta Braves, Joe called his starting pitchers into his office individually and asked them what the pitching rotation should be. Each one of them—David Cone, Roger Clemens, Orlando Hernandez, and Andy Pettitte—said that it was Joe's decision and that they'd be satisfied with whatever he decided. His order turned out to be Hernandez-Cone-Pettitte-Clemens, and no one complained. The Yankees swept the Braves in four straight games, on the way to a record 14 consecutive World Series wins. By gaining agreement and encouraging his players to take ownership, Joe made sure his pitching staff was all of one mind and all behind him.

Recently I was talking to a ballplayer about being positive. Some of you will remember him, but not by his real name, William Hayward Wilson. If you've heard of him, it's as "Mookie." Mookie Wilson came up with the New York Mets in 1980 and managed to play 12 years in the Major Leagues, which may not sound so impressive unless you know that it happens to be about three times the average duration for a Major League Baseball player. Mookie is best known for topping the ground ball that hit the infield dirt with tremendous over-spin and rolled through Bill Buckner's legs in Game 6 of the 1986 World Series.

That's Mookie's most famous moment, and I've talked to him about what was running through his mind when it happened. But I've always been more interested in the bigger picture, in how he succeeded in getting to and staying in the major leagues. He told me:

> To be honest with you, when I came to the big leagues I knew that I had to maintain my ability to hit the ball. But I felt that I made it not because of my hitting; that was not the reason I came to the big leagues. I came to the big leagues because of what I brought to a team—the energy, the unpredictability, the excitement on a team. I mean I never hit .300 in my life, not even in the minor leagues.
>
> I felt certain there were other areas that were more valuable for me. And I had to maintain those things. I didn't feel I had to hit .300 or had to be a better hitter. I felt the things I had to maintain were my base running and my defense. And up to this day I believe that's why I made it to the big leagues, and

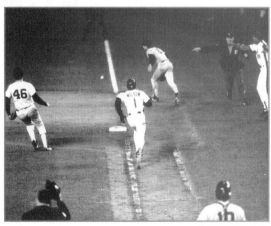

Mookie Wilson's ground ball scoots through the legs of Bill Buckner to score the winning run in Game 6 of the 1986 World Series.

Photo courtesy: Steiner Sports.

that's why I stayed here so long. It sure wasn't because of my hitting.

What Mookie was telling me was that he had found his niche; in fact, he found it before he was called up to the majors. His running, his energy—his ability to scamper around third and score from second base on a ground out—these were all part and parcel of the Wilson package and the key to his longevity. By the time he retired, he owned the Mets' record for steals with 281.

SEE OPPORTUNITY IN EVERY PHONE CALL

One of my firm's best relationships has been with American Express. That relationship started with my ringing phone.

Malcolm Goodrich, a top executive at American Express in the early '90s, was hosting a fund-raising event for the Boy Scouts and needed a couple of athletes to go on a boat ride around Manhattan and he needed them in a hurry, like in 48 hours. I didn't know who Malcolm was at the time, but I knew that this was the kind of thing Steiner Sports did best. I learned that he was a fan of the New York Giants and the Mets, so we called Sean Landeta, who won two Super Bowl rings with the Giants; Ottis Anderson, the Super Bowl XXV MVP; and Art Shamsky,

Running back Ottis Anderson of the New York Giants plows ahead during a game against the Los Angeles Rams at Giants Stadium in East Rutherford, New Jersey.

Photo courtesy: Getty Images.

who played on the Mets' 1969 World Championship team. We took them on the boat and brought along Earl Monroe for the basketball fans.

The event was a big success. It was a win-win situation for everyone. The athletes schmoozed, sold raffle tickets to the guests (who had paid $500 a ticket for the boat ride), and generally made themselves available to the fans. Having the players there made Malcolm look good, and it made Steiner Sports look good.

One thing you'll find about the people who occupy the seats of corporate power: They never forget a favor. For months on end, it seemed like all this man wanted to do was repay me for making him look good. I decided to let him, and it's been a win-win relationship ever since. Together we created some major programs for American Express and its customers. Steiner Sports organized Super Bowl parties for American Express for five years—one at the Playboy Mansion—and we got involved with the American Express Platinum Card. The company supplied motivational speakers for American Express managers across the country, and we established an ongoing premiere relationship with American Express Membership Rewards. That program has been good for the card members and great for Steiner Sports, exposing millions of people to our company every month.

With the Membership Rewards Program, a corporation approaches Steiner Sports with the idea of doing an incentive program for their employees. If the corporation reaches a sales quota Steiner Sports will hook them up with memorabilia to keep or resell. For example, if a tire dealership sells 100 tires in a certain amount of time, they get an autographed picture or a letter signed by, say, Derek Jeter, which would read, "Good job. Keep up the good work."

LOOK FOR NEW WAYS TO GROW

Our collectibles business came out of the idea of supporting the "celebrity appearances" side of our company. We started the collectibles side with a whopping $10,000 right out of the bank. We first saw it as a sideline, just a way to make more than our 15 percent fee and enhance an athlete appearance by bringing souvenir stuff to sell, but as the collectibles business grew, we recognized the potential, and now it's a $20 million-plus business on its own. It was a matter of expanding on the things that were already working. We weren't reinventing the wheel, just putting more spokes in it.

It was my partner Jared Weiss who was responsible for changing the nature of our business. Jared would accompany athletes on every appearance and was relentless in getting stuff signed. Jared might be next to Keith Hernandez on an appearance or to a signing show, and he'd say, "Keith, can you sign these 12 balls for me?" Or maybe he'd be in the back of a limo with hockey superstar Gordie Howe, stuck in traffic on the way to a speaking engagement. Jared would be sitting there with a duffle bag and ask Gordy to sign 100 sticks or pucks. It was no big deal then, but today it would cost us seven grand to get those 100 pieces autographed.

So by 1993 we had built up this enormous closet of inventory. And people would constantly call us and ask, "You got a Darryl Strawberry ball laying around?" "You got this?" "You got that?" People kept calling and calling and we decided, to start a memorabilia company.

From there, Jared's ingenuity took over. He's very creative with products for athletes. He decided then that we should have our own photo company. We have athletes sign a lot of photos. So his idea was not to farm out the photos but to do them in-house. Naturally, if you

Photo courtesy: Steiner Sports.

Brandon Steiner (left) with partner Jared Weiss.

create your own picture frames, display cases, and photos, you'll save substantial money.

Philosophically speaking, the decision to expand to memorabilia was the right one. Jared kept saying to me, "We've always been a customer-driven company, not a management-driven company." It's true: You have two choices to make. Do you want to be in the business that your management team decides you should be in? Or do you want to be in the business your customers say you should be in? And we've always been customer-driven. We know what our customers want and try to meet their needs.

BUILD TRUST AND KEEP TRUST

The trust and faith of other people is like a china cup. Once you break it, you can glue the pieces together, but it's never quite the same. It's easy to gain people's trust initially. Even hard-nosed business people are reasonably trusting. Maintaining that trust is another story. Of course I'm talking about honesty, but I'm talking about something much more delicate too—*the consistent belief that you will do what you say you will do.*

Once you make a promise, keep it. Author Stephen Covey was once asked, "How can a person build character?" He answered, "Make a promise. Then keep it. Then make another promise and keep that one."

Covey got it precisely right. Keep all your promises, however difficult that might be, whatever it may cost you. If nothing else, you'll learn not to make promises you can't keep! Like the great guitarist Bo Diddley once said, "Don't let your mouth write no check that your butt can't cash." Keep the little promises too, the ones that don't even seem like promises.

Aside from my mother, the person with probably the greatest influence on my attitude toward work and character was a man named Alzie Jackson, head chef of Camp Sussex in New Jersey for 25 years, and my boss every summer I worked in that camp kitchen. Alzie is no longer with us, but he'll always be with me in spirit.

I was the number-two man in the camp kitchen, which meant that I made all the soups and was responsible for making sure dinner service went properly. One day I was making cream of tomato soup from scratch, cooking down the tomatoes. I didn't like cream of tomato soup, and I still don't. I made friends on the wait staff just to get someone to taste my tomato soup, so I wouldn't have to do it myself! It was well over 100 degrees in that kitchen, and the sweat was just pouring off all of us. I think I was on my third T-shirt since breakfast. The tomatoes were all cooked down and I was heating the milk. For those of you who are not "soup-meisters," you must know that a cook has got to be careful to keep stirring the milk and not let it boil because milk scalds. If you pour scalded milk into tomato soup, you get some pretty unappetizing white spots floating around in there.

I scalded the milk. And I poured it into the soup.

I tried everything to get those little white dots out of the soup! I went fishing with a big spoon; I strained it, I tried wishing them away. No good. It looked like oversized mothballs had invaded my soup. I went up to Alzie and said, "We're not serving soup today."

Alzie, an imposing 6-foot-5-inch man, stood over me and smiled. "You must be crazy," he said. The man then made perfect tomato soup from scratch in 45 minutes, and I still don't know how he did it.

When he finished, he pulled me aside and said, "Brandon, the first time you don't deliver what's on the menu is when people lose faith in you. That's when you lose their trust." Alzie taught me dozens of life lessons just as simple—and just as profound.

Watch what the masses are doing, and do the opposite. Do good work and maintain your integrity. Develop consummate knowledge. Stay positive and keep positive people around you. Make a promise and keep it.

My mother (the greatest business mind I've ever known) used to say, "If you know how to do business, it doesn't matter whether you sell socks or stocks."

A champion becomes a champion for a reason, and the first step in becoming a champion is to know your reason, your "why."

Mom was right. I chose sports marketing because I saw an opportunity. Athletes were being undermarketed in the mid-1980s. I saw the opportunity because I love sports; I saw a way to combine my love and knowledge of sports with my ability to promote events and promote and market talent. Do what you love to do and what you know, whatever it is, and use what you learn in this book to lead you to success.

—— *Chapter Review* ——

▶ Find your niche and pursue it with passion.

▶ Stay positive and keep positive people around you.

▶ See what most people are doing, and do the opposite.

▶ The people who sit in the seats of corporate power never forget a favor.

▶ You don't have to reinvent the wheel—just put more spokes on it.

▶ If you know how to do business, it doesn't matter if you're selling socks or stocks.

Photo courtesy: Steiner Sports.

Coach Tom Landry with Roger Staubach. Landry was a mainstay in Dallas, coaching for 29 years.

What you do with your time is your legacy.

—Bob Feller, Hall of Fame pitcher and
winner of eight Battle Stars in World War II.

WAKE UP NERVOUS!

Reading the stories of great achievers is one of my favorite pastimes. I began watching the show *Biography* at an early age, rushing home from delivering newspapers to sit in front of the television to find out who Mike Wallace would be bringing to life today. One day it was Winston Churchill; on another, Queen Elizabeth; and another, Babe Ruth. I love learning about what drives these people, what leads them to achieve, and why.

In this chapter, I'll tell you a little about what drives me, about my "why," and ask you to start developing your why, to build that spark into a burning desire to succeed.

I love learning. Learning about the lives of great achievers can help you to start developing your "why" to build that spark into a burning desire to succeed. Hearing athletes and coaches describe in their own words how they've turned sparks into flames may help you build your own fire.

The late Tom Landry said, "The drive to succeed comes from inside." Landry played for the New York Giants, mostly on defense, from 1949 to 1955. He was a solid player, but he was one of those athletes who achieved far greater fame as a coach. Landry was the one with the familiar Stetson hat, patrolling the sidelines for the Dallas Cowboys from 1960 through 1988. The "Boys" were a perennial power and won five NFC championships and two Super Bowls (in 1972 and 1978) during his reign. His inner fire burned constantly for 29 years. There was no more steady individual in sports.

Jim Brown, who led the NFL in rushing in eight of his nine years, said, "I like to do the impossible."

Ernie Banks told me, "The successful people I've been around have such a different attitude than most people. They say, 'I like you guys and ladies, you're wonderful, but I come to *win*.'" Banks was a Hall of Fame shortstop for the Chicago Cubs whose career spanned three decades, from the 1950s to the 1970s. His ideas about attitude are what kept him going. After all, Ernie played with those perennial cellar dwellers, the Chicago Cubs. Despite their place in the basement of the National League, Banks took care of his game. The Baseball Writers of America noticed: Banks received the league's MVP award twice.

Then there's Bob Feller. This Hall of Fame hurler for the Cleveland Indians, this American patriot who enlisted in the Navy the day after the attack on Pearl Harbor in 1941, owns something special deep down. From my conversations with him, I have come to believe that the finer stuff has always been inside of him.

A genuine American hero, Feller, 84, speaks quickly, wanting to get all his words out, hoping someone will find them important. I do, and I think you will, too when you hear what he has learned about success.

"Kids playing baseball, or any sport—or doing anything in life— must have self-discipline. You need to say no to a lot of frivolous things

Bob Feller is congratulated after pitching one of the three no-hitters of his career on July 1, 1951.

Photo courtesy: Steiner Sports.

that waste your time. When you come on this earth, you're given so much time: What you do with your time is your legacy. You can throw it away or make good use of it. Lost time is never found. Thomas Edison said, 'Find out what you want to do early in life and then do it.'"

STAY NERVOUS

I'm asked to speak in front of groups of people fairly often. At a recent engagement, a meeting of Citibank managers and clients, one of the executives hosting the affair asked if I was nervous. I had to think about it. I scanned the dining room. This was a luncheon meeting, a roomful of investment bankers and investors, young and middle-aged men and women in navy blue and charcoal-gray suits who controlled a great deal of money and represented a lot of potential business for me. I turned to the host and answered, "Not really."

"Not really" didn't mean "no," it meant no more nervous than usual. I wake up nervous every morning! It's the excitement and energy that powers my day, and to be honest with you, it's excitement and passion mixed with a little fear. I think every successful man is a little afraid of losing what he's got, what he's built.

Sandy Koufax (also a Brooklyn boy) once said, "You know, sometimes the most terrified people do the best work." Koufax was the most

Sandy Koufax holds four balls, one for each no-hitter he threw. With the Los Angeles Dodgers, Koufax won three Cy Young Awards in 1963, 1965, and 1966. He was a two-time World Series Most Valuable Player in 1963 and 1965. His last no-hitter was a perfect game against the Chicago Cubs on September 9th, 1965.

Photo courtesy: Steiner Sports.

dominating pitcher of the early 1960s. But that doesn't do it justice. Sandy Koufax was just plain unhittable. He faced the best hitters in the league—guys like Willie Mays, Hank Aaron, and Frank Robinson —and he usually prevailed. He was forced to retire after the 1966 season, at 30, because of an arthritic left elbow. Five years later he became the youngest inductee into the Hall of Fame.

Despite Koufax's greatness, most people don't realize that Sandy had a fear of crowds. Imagine pitching in Chavez Ravine, before 54,000 Los Angeles Dodgers fans, and suffering from a fear of crowds! I don't think that large a dose of terror is the way to go, but a little edge of fear keeps me focused, and the nervous energy gives a boost to everything I do throughout a busy day.

The Great One, Wayne Gretzky, also had fear. "A fear of failure drives the great athletes," Gretzky said. Can you imagine that? Gretzky is the all-time NHL leader in goals, assists, and points. What else is there? The man with the number 99 on his jersey is regarded as the best by everyone who knows the game. Yet he was driven to succeed by a fear of failure. Fear can drive you, too.

When you wake up each day, you can't be passive about that day's possibilities. The day owes us nothing. In fact, we owe the day. What do we owe it? We owe it effort. Looked at in this way, our waking hours take on a different color. That attitude creates a nervous buzz.

ROLLING WITH THE NERVES

U sing that nervous energy can really improve your perform- ance. One example I think of is Phil Rizzuto on the day he was inducted into the Baseball Hall of Fame in 1994. Rizzuto was such a beloved player in New York. He was the shortstop for the New York Yankees from 1941 to 1956. During his time with the Bronx Bombers they won ten pennants and

Photo courtesy: Getty Images.

eight World Series, including a record five World Series in a row from 1949 to 1953. Just 5-feet-6 and 150 pounds, he was known as "The Scooter" for his speed. After his retirement, he spent 39 years in the broadcast booth and became famous for bellowing "Holy Cow"—usually when a Yankee player did something that amazed him. When the action slowed down, he would talk about which Italian bakeries sold the best cannoli or rap with partner Bill White about how to make pesto sauce.

Arguments raged about whether Rizzuto belonged in the Hall of Fame. For 15 years the Baseball Writers Association passed over him. After that period, a player's fate rests with the Veterans Committee. After an agonizing 11-year wait, the committee elected him.

It was a joyous time for Phil and his family and I had introduced him to about five different speechwriters, and we had finally found just the person to write his speech, one of the best sports writers for such occasions. Scooter was well prepared but so nervous that you couldn't talk to him for days before the ceremony. When the time arrived, I was sitting with Phil and his wife, Cora, and 20,000 other people at the Hall of Fame in Cooperstown, New

York. I said, "Phil, are you OK?" He said, "Brandon, I'm so nervous I don't know what to do."

But when he was introduced, Phil walked up to the podium and gave one of the best Hall of Fame speeches of all time. He used none of what the writer had given him—he went with his gut and his instincts—and all of his favorite stuff came to mind. He tallked about how his mother pinned a $20 bill to the inside of his shirt, so it wouldn't be stolen, the first time he went to the South to play minor league baseball. He talked about receiving a white mass of food for breakfast, not knowing what it was, until someone told him it was grits. From there, it was nonstop laughter.

You know, sometimes you've got to be nervous to be good. I had never seen anyone as nervous as Phil had been about getting into the Hall, even after 39 years of talking to millions on radio and television. There had been so much controversy about his going in and now, ten years after the election of Pee Wee Reese, the shortstop for the rival Dodgers in the '40s and '50s, Phil had been elected. With all that scuttlebutt surrounding him, he got up there and gave one of the funniest, best—and longest—speeches of all time. I can't remember a more enjoyable moment. Phil had all these writers

helping him, but he ended up going off the cuff. It was totally Scooter. So that's why I say that sometimes you've got to be nervous to be good. You've got to see nervousness for what it is— energy.

Photo courtesy: AP Worldwide.

Different things motivate different people. Dale Carnegie said one of the strongest drives of all human beings is the drive to feel important. People sometimes identify Carnegie's idea with the need for "existential meaning." Exactly what that is can vary from person to person.

DO IT ANYWAY

Frank Robinson is a man of "firsts and onlys." First and only MLB player to be named MVP in both leagues, first and only player to hit 200 home runs in both leagues, first African American manager in the major leagues, and the only Black man to manage in both leagues. I asked Frank how he handled being the first, what he did about that voice within that says, "You can't do it, it's never been done."

> I handle it by not thinking about it. You keep the focus on the situation at hand, and let everything take care of itself. My first manager, Birdie Tebbetts, taught me how to do that, by challenging me to do things he knew I could do and not pressuring me to do them. I carried that with me through the rest of my career.

I asked New York Yankee star Derek Jeter how he could top being in five World Series, winning the World Series MVP against the rival Mets in 2000, and being a day-in-day-out matinee idol in New York. He said, "I don't think about what I've already done. It's not even in my mind. I focus on the present, and worry about what's going to happen in the future."

Another big lesson: *do it anyway*. None of us is fearless. We all get nervous; we all have the tendency to procrastinate. Procrastination comes from fear. Once you have a plan, push forward. Get moving. If you're afraid you might fail, do it anyway. Hey, even if you're afraid you might succeed, do it anyway!

SEE THE LIGHT

I often say that I was very lucky in life to have seen the light at an early age. Of course, in my case, it was the refrigerator light, shining very brightly, because we didn't have much food!

To me, "seeing the light" is being motivated. In every endeavor, whether it's sports, business, or mowing your lawn, you need to be motivated. Seeing the light is keeping your eyes on the prize; it's knowing why you want to make things happen. It's pretty easy to get motivated and pumped up. The real challenge of the champion is to stay motivated. Seeing the light is looking into that empty refrigerator, hungry, be grateful for whatever you have, but be willing to do whatever it takes to get the things you need and want.

Harry Carson, a former New York Giants linebacker, said, "I only know how to play at one speed—full out." Harry was always a strongly motivated player. A fourth-round draft pick out of South Carolina State University, he had to be committed first to make the team and then to stay in the NFL. "You have to improve upon just about everything; your physical conditioning, everything. But for me, it was solely about commitment. I think some people go into situations not fully committed, or they don't know what kind of commitment it takes to be successful." Harry Carson not only stayed in the league 13 years—which is three times longer than the NFL's four-year average—but was All Pro six times and played on a Super Bowl winner in 1987.

STAY ON TOP OF YOUR GAME

Every time I meet with Derek Jeter, I'm enormously impressed with his level of motivation. I sat down with Derek during the late fall of 1999 and asked him where he was vacationing. I assumed he was going to relax— he'd just won his third World Series in four years with the team, and the '99 season had been his best year so far. I figured he'd hang at some resort and sip margueritas. "So, Derek," I asked, "Where are you gonna go?"

Derek Jeter throwing from deep in the hole at short-stop.

Photo courtesy: Getty Images.

"Go?" Derek answered with an excited gleam in his eye. "I'm working out every day—spring training is just around the corner!" He looked hungry, as if there was a chance he might not make the team the following season. Derek was letting me know that vacations aren't a priority when you're striving to stay on top of your game. He even moved out of New York City so he wouldn't be sidetracked by the nightlife and distracted from his game.

Guess who has more base hits than any player in baseball since 1996? Derek Jeter.

DO YOUR HOMEWORK

Any quarterback in the NFL will tell you, unequivocally, that the greatest quarterbacks have always been the ones who are the best students. You can't be a great quarterback unless you study game films religiously. And the greatest coaches are the ones who can teach their quarterbacks how to watch films—how to be a good student.

A great example of a student of sport has to be Joe Gibbs. An incredible workaholic of a football coach, Joe never stopped watching films of the game. This guy outworked, outlearned, and outstudied anybody in the league, and it helped him take the Washington Redskins to several Super Bowls.

Doc Rivers talks about this kind of preparation and relates it to defensive play. Rivers was a heady NBA guard who played his best years with the Atlanta Hawks and New York Knicks. He took his court smarts with him to the sideline and became coach of the Orlando Magic. "Find the spot your opponent likes to shoot from, and get there first," Rivers said, when someone asked him about his thinking on the court. "If you know what your prospect's tendencies are, you can be at the right place at the right time."

The man they called "Mr. Hockey," Gordie Howe, once told me, "If you wanna be the best and be inspired to do more with your career, then your work has to be like a love affair."

I'll do you one better. Cal Ripken retired from baseball in 2001 after 21 seasons. He long ago wrote his ticket to the Hall of Fame and owns a record of playing in 2,632 consecutive games, a record that we will almost surely never see broken. I asked him if he ever had to increase his training to achieve something new or overcome some bad habits.

There were certain times when I felt that I needed to dedicate myself in the off-season a little bit more to get in the best shape that I possibly could get into. Sometimes I would have an injury or two that would cause me to focus more in the off-season. But I tried to be as honest as I could with myself. And halfway through my career, during the off-season in 1990, I remember thinking, "OK, I don't know how long my career will last. I'm halfway through. I'm 30 years old . . ." I had struggled a little bit the year before and Frank Robinson helped right me from a hitting standpoint and trying to get back to the way I was swinging the bat before. And I thought, "OK, this is the off-season to make everything come together. I'm going to work really hard and I'm going to become the best shape I've been and go in the next season with the skills stuff in the right place and also the physical side in the right place." And it turned out to be my best year ever. That was 1991.

Cal won his second Most Valuable Player Award that year.

DON'T REST ON YOUR LAURELS

NBA coach Pat Riley talked about the complacency that crept into the Los Angeles Lakers' locker room after the team won a championship in 1985. The team had defeated the Celtics and a decades-old jinx of losing to Boston in the finals. They even clinched the series in Boston, on the Celtics' parquet floor. In the 1985–86 season, however, the team seemed to gloat about its own success. In Riley's words, "The temptation to slack off starts when you're feeling good about who you are and what you've achieved." As a result, the team didn't dig as deep and ended

up losing in the playoffs to Houston in 1986. Complacency had beaten the Lakers, just as surely as Hakeem Olajuwon and the Rockets had.

I do my best to apply that lesson. Steiner Sports' best year ever was 1999: we doubled our sales over the previous year and we *quadrupled* our profits, maintaining the same overhead! It was the

Miami Heat head coach Pat Riley signals during a pre-season game against the Dallas Mavericks at the Miami Arena. This is Riley's first appearace at the arena as head coach for the Miami Heat.

Photo courtesy: AP Worldwide.

kind of year that any company would dream of. We were challenged; everybody made the most of our opportunities. And in the last week of the year, it was time to party.

Human nature says that when you've had a success, it's time to ease up and enjoy it. My way of doing things is to take the momentum of that success and use it to push me ahead to the next one.

While my staff celebrated, I left the party and began to plan for the year 2000. In fact, I canceled my vacation and spent that last week of the year doing what I really love—figuring out how we were going to do even better! I believe that true competitors never want to miss a beat or fall behind. I believe that to stay in front of the pack, you need to develop one of two abilities: the ability to plan while you celebrate or the ability to walk away from the celebration before everyone else does. If you can't do either, then I suggest you postpone the celebration until you've reached the top.

It reminded me of being in the Hard Rock Cafe in 1985 on a late Saturday night. I was an assistant manager, and it was the most successful night we'd had up to that point; every celebrity who was in New York at that time was at the Hard Rock. I was walking the floor noticing everything that could be improved. At 4:30 in the morning, following an 11-hour shift, when all 90 employees were counting their money and dreaming of hurrying home, I called a meeting, discussing everything they could have done better. I had a great staff, and no one blinked an eye.

They were beyond tired but stayed and listened for the better part of an hour. I told them how they could do even better by helping each other out, by assisting a colleague who was overwhelmed with the pace by busing a table, or taking a bill to the cashier. The following weekend, with nowhere near the same volume of business or hectic pace, the staff made more money because they took the lessons to heart and worked more efficiently.

—— *Chapter Review* ——

▶ Know your reason for achieving success.

▶ Stay nervous.

▶ See the light. Stay motivated by keeping your "why" in front of you.

▶ Stay on top of your game.

▶ Don't rest too early.

Centers Mark Messier and Wayne Gretzky of the New York Rangers hug each other during a playoff game against the Florida Panthers at the Miami Arena in Miami, Florida. The Rangers won the game 3 to 2.

*O*ne of the things I took pride in was that some of my teammates in Baltimore, because of my consecutive games streak, actually felt a bigger obligation to go out there and play for the sake of the team. Several players had some of their best years and played every single game; they took pride in being there for their team.

—Cal Ripken, former shortstop for the Baltimore Orioles
who set a record for consecutive games played.

KNOW YOUR PURPOSE

We have already talked about setting goals. Once specific goals have been set, you need to turn your attention to the even more important step of finding your purpose. Whereas a goal is directed toward yourself and your own activity, a purpose is directed outward. A goal answers the question, "What do I want and when do I want it?"—a purpose answers the question, "What am I here for?" or "What am I supposed to be doing?"

Now, before you say to yourself, "Oh, here's where Brandon lays on me that philosophical-religious-New-Age-touchy-feely stuff," let me assure you that we're not going there. Like everything else in this book, it's simpler—I'll give you the answer. In fact, I've already given you the answer. You and I and the guy down the block are all here to meet the needs of other people. I believe that's our purpose, and so far no one's been able to prove me wrong. Every little bit of happiness in my life (as well as every dollar I've made) has come from meeting the needs of other people. If you think about it for a moment, the same holds true for you. Many great minds have agreed: The only way to get other people to give you what you want is to give them what they want. Now, if that's our purpose in life, isn't it simpler to get in line with that purpose instead of ignoring it, or worse, going against it?

Fundamental to this purpose is caring. Caring about other people, caring about what they need and want, and doing what you can to meet those needs and wants. Now, I can't make you care about other people. But you'd better start learning how to care and practice it, if you want to keep it simple and live as a champion.

Let's start thinking in terms of something I learned from Dr. Spencer Johnson's book, *The One Minute Sales Person.* Johnson suggests looking at things in a way that I call "The Tombstone Effect." What would you hope to have written on your tombstone?

HERE LIES JOE—HE SPENT ALL HIS TIME
MAKING MONEY

or

HERE LIES JOE—HE ALWAYS CARED FOR OTHERS

I've never heard of anyone who at the end of his life said, "You know, I should have cared more about myself."

One of my favorite glimpses of someone focusing on the needs of others was of Mark Messier, right after the New York Rangers won the Stanley Cup, the National Hockey League's championship trophy. Maybe you can imagine how the Rangers were going crazy—it was their first Stanley Cup in 54 years. Suddenly, Mark pulled everybody together in the locker room and said, "Listen, there's no better moment than this one, but we are not bigger than life. Here's the 800-number to the limousine service that I use. I don't want anybody driving if you're drinking; we're not bigger than that. So call this number, I'll never ask you a question about it, and you have somebody drive you to wherever you need to go. You're going to be celebrating, you don't need to be driving."

Mark didn't stop there. "And let's not forget all the equipment people and the locker-room boys," he added, "because they've been with us through this long run, and in a way they won a Stanley Cup, too, but they don't get a piece of all the money we're getting. Let's make sure we tip them, don't forget to tip them, and tip them big, because they busted their humps, too." That is classic Messier: stopping in the middle of all the joy and bedlam and thinking of others.

In fact, Messier is one of the greatest "recognizers" I know. When Mark walks into Steiner Sports, he greets everyone—from the receptionist to the stockpersons in my warehouse—with the same smile, the same handshake, and the same friendly attitude. Mark is good at remembering names, too. He lets everyone around know that they are all important to him, because they're people. When Mark invites the people in my office somewhere, he doesn't just invite the big shots. He invites EVERYONE. And everyone in the office thinks very highly of Mr. Messier because he takes the time to recognize them all.

PLAYING THE ODDS

It occurs to me at this point that some of you might be thinking, "These are lovely sentiments, Brandon, but what about all those people who go through life taking advantage of other people, like the ones who get rich without giving a damn about the other guy?"

Well, first of all, we're not talking about them. We're talking about you, and me, and all the other true champions. In fact, even the people who don't care have to serve others in some way in order to get anywhere. They're just doing it the hard way, without caring or considering the basic elements of what they're doing.

Keep in mind, however, that not everyone is playing by the same rules. Not everyone you treat well will treat you well, and not everyone

Positive Support

I once had a rare opportunity to talk with basketball legend Bill Russell. Bill didn't want to talk about his 11 championship rings in 13 NBA seasons, or his two NCAA championships with San Francisco. Bill wanted to talk about his Boston Celtics coach Red Auerbach, and especially about Red's talent for establishing immediate credibility with his players.

Russell said his college coach had done a great job, but he had never really felt a personal connection with that coach, never felt like they were really on the same page. But on one of his first nights as a Celtic, Bill committed a marginal foul, and Auerbach ran onto the court and began arguing with the referee. Auerbach thought the call was a good one, but he wanted to let Russell know he was the kind of coach who would always watch his player's back and fight for him. Bill Russell said that moment cemented their relationship immediately—knowing that Red Auerbach would go to the wall for him inspired Russell to feel the same way about Auerbach.

Is it any wonder that Auerbach, known as "The Great Motivator," had the right stuff to lead his troops to nine World Championships from 1957 to 1966? Red would come into training camp in the fall and ask them, "Did you have a good summer? Did everyone pat you on the back for winning last spring? Well, all it takes is for you to have two consecutive bad games, and they'll be calling you bums.'"

The players got the message. Rather than allowing them to rest on their laurels, Red always inspired them to grab for new ones. In a word, he supported his players; in return, they gave back.

Auerbach wouldn't browbeat his troops or tell them what to do at key points in the game. Instead he would huddle them and ask for their help. He would say things like, "Can you control the defensive boards here? Can anyone help me get this rebound? Cause I think if we control the boards for these last few possessions, we're going to win this game."

Remember that your employees, your coworkers, and most important your family, would all appreciate that kind of support from you. When someone comes to you with a problem, sometimes you need to step up and show them that you'll support them unconditionally. That kind of support comes back to you again and again.

Photo courtesy: Getty Images.

Coach Red Auerbach (left) and Bill Russell. Together with the Boston Celtics, they won every NBA championship from 1959 to 1966.

you share with will share with you. But to quote Damon Runyon, "That's the way to bet." If you do good, you'll get good. It may not come from the direction you think it should, but it will come. And plentifully. Ralph Waldo Emerson called it "The Law of Compensation." I call it caring.

CULTIVATING A FAN CLUB

A big part of becoming successful, besides doing your best, is having the people around you feel good about you. The athletes I've talked to agree that your biggest fans should be people closest to you. You can't go around tooting your own horn. No matter how big you are, how big a player, how much money you're making, you still can't promote yourself. The most important thing, whether you're an entrepreneur, an employee, or an athlete, is to always strive to do the best you can yourself. The people around you will notice, whether you realize it or not.

Others should toot your horn the loudest. The highest praise about the greatest sports stars comes mostly from their teammates. NBA superstar Larry Bird didn't talk about how great he was or how many passes he gave to other players or how he helped everyone on the team look good. It was up to his Boston Celtics teammates to say, "When Larry's got the ball you never know what's going to happen; he's always thinking of everyone else." You know that Robert Parrish and Kevin McHale, who played on that front line with him, got a lot more easy shots with Larry playing "point-forward"—feeding them the ball. People described Bird's function this way, because he played forward but usually had the ball like a point guard. And Dennis Johnson had the chance to shoot many more open jumpers when defenses double-teamed Bird. He made the game easier for his teammates, and they knew it and talked about it.

In business, wouldn't it be great if you could turn the people you deal with into salespeople for you? If you had your own fan club made up of your friends, coworkers, and clients? What if every person you came in contact with walked away with a good feeling about you, good enough so they'd tell others how great you are?

This is what creates the aura of greatness. You need to make sure you're thinking of others often and helping them out, so your coworkers become your fan club.

BUILD A WINNING TEAM

Real leadership also means being aware of what the people around you need. Try to know your people (family, friends, coworkers) well enough

APPRAISAL FROM YOUR OWN

A nother story about recognition from others comes to mind. Bill Walton is an NBA broadcaster. Before that he played center for two teams that won championships, the Portland Trailblazers and then the Boston Celtics. He was voted into the Basketball Hall of Fame in 1993. Of all the things that have been said about him, the one he says he remembers best is something from Portland teammate Maurice Lucas.

"Moe" Lucas was a give-no-quarter tough guy. He earned a rep around the league as "The Enforcer" for the way he wielded his elbows and shoulders while rebounding. In the middle of the Trailblazers' championship run. In 1977, he told Bill, "You help your teammates play better basketball." Says Walton, "It was the nicest thing anybody ever said about me as a player. No one made me a better player than Maurice Lucas. His toughness, his leadership, his commitment to the team, is off the charts."

Why did Walton remember the sentiment more than a quarter of a century after Portland won its title? It was an appraisal from one of his own, from someone who had the same goals to win a title as he had. Simply put, it was the recognition of a peer.

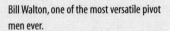

Bill Walton, one of the most versatile pivot men ever.

Photo courtesy: Getty Images.

so you know when they're "off their game," when they need some help without their having to ask. Ideally, you won't just ask if they need help either, you will be specific. "Can I give you a hand with the research on the XYZ project?" is a more sincere and helpful approach than, "Hey, any of you guys need any help?"

Frank Robinson says, "If you start to focus on the individual accomplishments, trying to accomplish something outside of the frame of the team, you're going to run into trouble."

As I said in an earlier chapter, when Cal Ripken wasn't swinging the bat well after the 1990 season, it was Frank Robinson who showed him what adjustments he could make to his swing. With that fine-tuning, Ripken was off and running, enjoying his own personal renaissance, and earning his second MVP award.

John Wooden, who coached the UCLA Bruins basketball team from 1949 to 1975, said, "In all my years of coaching, my players never heard me use the word 'winning.' I wanted winning to be the by-product of something even more important: the constant quest to be the best we were capable of being. It's not easy advice to follow, but if you do follow it, winning more often than not takes care of itself." That attitude, that focus, that *sense of purpose*, helped Wooden to lead UCLA to ten NCAA championships in 12 years, 16 conference championships, and 4 undefeated seasons.

Wooden was the "philosopher coach." Picture a practice at UCLA—Wooden running up and down the sidelines, a program rolled tight in his fist, barking out his instructions, motivational nuggets, and time-tested maxims: "Be quick, but don't hurry." "Failing to prepare is preparing to fail." "Never mistake activity for achievement." "Discipline yourself and others won't need to." It was exhilarating for his players, but the message wasn't about individuals. "You are part of something larger," he seemed to be saying. "You are not isolated. Your attempts at excellence will be felt by others."

His message resonates still. His greatest disciples are people such as Bill Walton and Kareem Abdul-Jabbar, Bob Costas, and Denny Crum, and so many others who have been touched by his personal wisdom.

Walton played for Wooden from 1971 through 1974 and counted those years as special. "My whole life I dreamed of being part of a special team, and there were always forces pushing me in the direction of individual goals, including the atmosphere and environment that I grew up in as a kid," Walton says. "But *every* coach I ever played for was a disciple of John Wooden and the team game." Until he got to the professional ranks with the Portland Trailblazers.

> When I got to the NBA in the '70, I was blown away by the selfishness and individualism and the greediness—it was a very tough introduction for me, and it wasn't until my third year in the league, when they made a lot of personnel changes and got a lot of team players in there, that we became the youngest team in the history of the NBA to win the championship.
>
> John Wooden never talked about winning and losing. He always talked about life's great lessons, about human values and personal characteristics you would need. It was the effort to win and to succeed and the search for excellence that just made it a glorious atmosphere. It was always fun and always upbeat, always at an incredibly fierce pace, but it was jovial and positive and always constructive. There was never any negativity, never any brow beating. It was never about him but always about the team and the greatness of the game of basketball.

John Wooden got the message across that the team was more important than the individual. His players learned the "Wooden Philosophy" and used it throughout their lives.

"John Wooden is the greatest college coach of all time," Walton told me. "But what I learned from him had much more to do with living than with playing ball." Among other things, Wooden left his players with an unceasing desire for excellence, which they in turn give to others, and they to others, moving continually outward like ripples in a pond.

Long after John Wooden is gone, he will be giving still.

GIVING WITH SENSITIVITY

Walt Frazier is a friend with whom I have been through thick and thin. Walt really understands the importance of meeting the needs of others. Frazier, of course, is the Hall of Fame basketball player who held New York in the palm of his hand when he led the Knicks to World Championships in 1970 and 1973. I make a lot of appearances with Walt Frazier, and he has always impressed me as someone who is sensitive to the needs of others. I want to tell you about one instance I just can't forget.

In my neighborhood outside of New York City, there was such devastation, such unimaginably great personal loss, after the terrorist attacks on September 11, 2001. More than 2,800 people were murdered in a space of minutes, which is just too horrible to contemplate. Those losses will be felt forever. Boys and girls lost their mothers and fathers, parents lost their sons and daughters—every variety of tragedy resulted from that one morning. Several neighborhoods—especially in Long Island, Westchester County, and New Jersey—were hit especially hard. In my neighborhood, one boy I know lost his father. I knew the boy because he played on the Little League team that I coached. I wanted to do something for him on his upcoming 11th birthday. I asked Walt if he could come and visit the boy for a while. I barely got the words out of my mouth before Walt agreed.

He drove up to the boy's house, on time, played basketball with him, and asked him about his hobbies and how he was doing. What really impressed me is how Walt remembered that it was the boy's birthday and took the time to purchase a watch for him. I don't have to tell you how thrilled this kid was. For an hour, he forgot his troubles, which were pretty significant. He knew that Walt was the Knicks broadcaster on the Madison Square Garden channel, and now he had a chance to play with Walt and get his autograph. When I think of what Walt did, and the completely gracious way in which he did it, I'm touched still.

THE STEINER SPORTS TEAM

To keep all these balls in the air, I've had to team up with some talented, hungry people who are willing to play an important role for the good of the whole. One is Margaret Adams. Margaret came to us from the music and entertainment business where she booked some of the top bands in the country. At Steiner Sports, she is director of player relations. She's intuitive about matching the right kind of athlete to a customer's needs. Some company manager might say, "I want this star for an appearance ..."and insist on getting athlete X to make an appearance. Margaret might tell them, "I think I know someone who will work better with your group." Now, the customer is paying, so they can have whoever they want. But many of them have come back to her and said, "You know, I wish I'd taken your advice; that guy we signed just didn't interact well with our group." Whether it's music or sports, you need someone who can sense what's needed and who also has the rapport with clients and is trusted by them. Margaret has the goods.

In our business, you also need to keep new and different products coming out. Even the most avid collectors get tired of the same merchandise. The business has changed in the last couple of decades; it isn't just about baseball cards and pictures any more. Cliff Savage is our vice president of new product development and sales. He was with Franklin sporting goods for 15 years before that. Cliff invented nonautographed licensed products that get into Kmart, Target, and Toys "R" Us stores. He was a childhood friend from Brooklyn, and to be truthful, I never thought of him being a salesperson, but he's brilliant at it. He developed our stadium pools—little swimming pools for kids with likenesses of ballparks such as Fenway Park and Yankee Stadium in them. He also devised our Star-lights, a small toy you look into, the same way you would look into a kaleidoscope, and see a lighted likeness of Derek Jeter or some such star player, and a miniature version that you can plug into a socket as a night-light. Just like his father, Dr. Savage, the optician, Cliff's an inventor.

If you have a large stable of athletes, as we do, you need someone who can make that contact and keep the athletes happy. Matt Lalin is our vice president of athlete relations. He hunts down business on ath-letes and represents players for all their marketing. He signed on Ozzie Smith, the recent Hall of Famer, and will be handling all Ozzie's appear-ances for us. He does the same for Gary Carter, who was elected to the Hall in 2003. He also listens to what the customers need and goes and gets it. You rarely hear Matt say, "I can't do that."

Then there's Jared Weiss. As I told you in Chapter 2, Jared was responsible for changing the nature of our business. Jared has been with me since 1992. He's now my number-two guy, and for people who need titles—I don't—he's the executive vice president. Among other things, his job is to supervise about two dozen people in the sales department. He has great relationships with athletes, and he's creative with products for athletes.

These are just a few of our key people. Without them and about 85 others, the company wouldn't be what it is today. The saying in sports is that there is no "I" in team. It's a cliché, but like many clichés, it's undeniably true. You can't have that group dynamic known as "syner-gism" unless you have a dynamic group—one that can work together for the common goal of bettering the company.

WINNING WITH YOUR TEAM

There are plenty of examples of synergism in sports, but the one that comes immediately to mind is the World Champion 1998 Yankees team. That squad won 114 games, and yet it has often been said that there was

"I guarantee we'll win the Super Bowl"! That was the famous quote from quarterback Joe Namath before the New York Jets Super Bowl III match-up against the heavily-favored Baltimore Colts. True to his prediction, Namath led the Jets to the greatest Super Bowl upset of all time.

Photo courtesy: Steiner Sports.

no one superstar who towered over the rest. Do you know how many Yankees hit 30 homers on that team? The answer might surprise you: none. The team won because each person played a vital part and together they made a great team.

Every sports fan over 40 knows the story of Joe Namath and the triumph of the American Football League in Super Bowl III, back in 1969. To refresh your memory, the Baltimore Colts had run through everyone in the National Football League with a record of 13 to 1. Green Bay had won the previous two Super Bowls in walkovers, and no one but no one gave any AFL team, including the New York Jets, a ghost of a chance. Las Vegas odds-makers favored Baltimore by 18 points, the largest margin ever given to a team in the history of the Super Bowl.

In the week leading up to the game, Namath was at a press conference where someone yelled out that the Jets had no chance. Namath shot back at the heckler, "Hey, we're going to win this game." It was a brash statement by Namath, who was responding to the insult to get some respect for his team. But he firmly believed it. As it turned out, he was right. The Colts were uptight, making mistake after mistake, and the Jets dominated, winning 16 to 7. I talked to Joe about it and he said:

> That prediction, that wasn't just about me. I wasn't doing it to draw attention to myself. That was a belief in our people. I knew

our guys were right. I was talking about our team, I wasn't talking about Joe Namath, saying he's gonna do this, that, or the other. That was us. We were getting no respect, and I wanted people to know that we were good, too. We weren't just showing up there to get beaten.

Namath was defending his team, supporting them. That belief in them didn't hurt. Jets' back Matt Snell ran wild, and the defense stopped every Colt drive but one. When the Colts finally scored in the fourth quarter, the game was essentially over already.

WINNING IN LIFE

I think I've driven home the point about meeting the needs of others, but I want to leave with the story of one man who just may have been our greatest philanthropist of the previous century. I'm talking about Albert Schweitzer, whose life was dedicated to serving others.

Albert Schweitzer was born in 1875 in Alsace, France. I'm leaving some details out, but at the age of 24, he received a Ph.D. in philosophy from the University of Strasbourg in Berlin. He enjoyed a kind of dual career, because he studied the life and music of Johann Sebastian Bach and even developed expertise as an organ maker.

But his interest in theology and philosophy led him, as he put it, "to make my life my argument," and he returned to the university to study medicine. Degree in hand, he set out to found a small hospital in a region then known as French Equatorial Africa. A half a century later, The Hospital of Albert Schweitzer in Lambarene, in the Gabon, attained the reputation of a shrine. Although the hospital was rather crude and hardly modern in its facilities and technology, it attracted doctors and nurses and assorted volunteers from the world over, all of whom would forego modern conveniences for a chance to work alongside *Le Grand Docteur* in treating thousands upon thousands of Africans.

Bear in mind that Schweitzer didn't want a lavish modern hospital. He wanted African villagers to feel comfortable in modest surroundings. He also realized that family connections were strong among Africans. In fact, they would shun a hospital in which sick patients would be separated from their relatives. To accommodate them, he examined the patients, provided prescriptions, and set them up in small huts similar to those they inhabited. Then the family members would care for the sick, following the instructions of the hospital staff.

Amazingly, the recovery rate at his hospital compared favorably with the best hospitals in the West. Schweitzer was a trailblazer, knowing that for patients to heal, they needed to feel confidence in their doctors and themselves. Lucky for the world, Albert Schweitzer lived until he was 90. Personal happiness was far less important for him than serving others. As Norman Cousins wrote of him, "He was willing to make an ultimate sacrifice for a moral principle."

If anyone ever understood and lived out the idea of helping others, it was Albert Schweitzer. Civilization would count itself fortunate to have other leading lights shining as brightly as he.

—— *Chapter Review* ——

▶ A purpose is bigger than a goal—and more important. Ask yourself, "Why am I here? What am I supposed to be doing?"

▶ The primary purpose of life, and the source of all reward, is meeting the needs of other people.

▶ The only way to get others to give you what you want is to give them what they want. It won't work every time, but the percentages will always be on your side.

▶ Caring about the needs of others is the secret of all success and happiness.

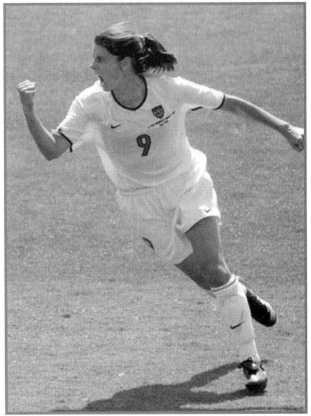

United States forward Mia Hamm celebrates her successful penalty kick against China during the final of the 1999 FIFA Women's World Cup at the Rose Bowl in Pasadena, California on July 10, 1999. The United States won the championship on the fifth shot of the penalty kick shoot-out.

If you go for the goal, like we did on the National Team, you'll always be going for a higher place. Each victory is great in and of itself, but champions are on a never-ending quest.

—Mia Hamm, who first competed for the United States National Team
at age 15 and has been on it ever since.

GO THE
EXTRA MILE

When I was a kid in Brooklyn, I had a paper route. I remember I started out with 39 daily and 45 Sunday papers. I'd get up before dawn, and my mom would help me fold and rubber-band the papers or bag them in plastic if the day was wet. I'd ride my bike down the street at six in the morning and wing the papers onto the lawns of my customers. On many mornings, it would eat me up that I was passing houses full of people who hadn't ordered the paper. I had to ride by their houses anyway, but I wasn't making a dime for it. So I thought about what it might take to get them to order the paper.

Then something dawned on me. Here it was the early 1970s, and there hadn't been a milkman in the neighborhood for as long as I could remember, yet almost everyone still drank milk every day. One day, when I was making my collections, I stopped at the houses that weren't taking the paper, and made them an offer. "If you start ordering the paper, I'll deliver a quart of milk with it every morning, and a loaf of bread when you want it. What do you say?" Now the convenience of having a paper delivered with milk was very appealing to many former customers.

Before I knew it, I had doubled the number of dailies and tripled the number of Sunday papers on my route.

My point is this: figure out what people want and give it to them. Do more than anyone else and you'll get more than anyone else. It occurs to me that *too many people stop looking for work once they've found a job*. Don't worry that you're working harder than other people.

THE SUCCESSFUL PERSON IS THE ONE WHO DOES WHAT THE UNSUCCESSFUL PERSON IS UNWILLING TO DO

If you're reading this book, you probably don't have a paper route any more. So? You work in an office, or you're out in the field selling, or you're a lineman for the telephone company. Find a way to do more, and to do more simply. If you're getting yourself a cup of coffee, ask your boss if he or she wants one. Bring your customer a doughnut or at least a smile. If you can't figure out what your customers want, ask them. And then give it to them. Then give some more. Some people think that's brown-nosing. I disagree; I think it is consideration. I think it's caring. I think it's building a reputation for excellence.

Baseball Hall of Famer Stan Musial says, "In any line of work, records you set will ultimately be broken—but a reputation for excellence will endure forever."

In interviewing athletes, you discover that some go the extra mile. Some really dig deep to tell you a story or give their opinion on an issue they know is important. Bob Feller, despite being 84 years old, talked to everyone who wanted to talk to him.

Another person who was happy to give above and beyond what was expected of him was baseball legend Mickey Mantle. I had the privilege of working with Mickey while he was still with us, making a number of personal appearances, speeches, and business promotions with him. You might think someone who had achieved the celebrity stature of "The Great Number Seven," as the late broadcaster Mel Allen referred to him on Mantle's retirement day, could just rest on his laurels, show up, and collect his fee.

But he didn't. Long after his career was over, he would sit in a booth at Mickey Mantle's Restaurant in New York City. When people would see him, they invariably wanted to say hello or get his autograph or have their pictures taken with him. For that purpose, Mantle kept a blue pen and a stack of postcards with a watercolor likeness of himself at his table. When people approached, he would sign the postcards for customers, just so they would have a keepsake. It wasn't any big deal. But it was something that any patron could tell their friends about. Mick signed so many of them that I still see them displayed in people's homes.

When it came to public appearances, Mickey always made sure people were satisfied with the job he was

Regarded as having the greatest combination of speed and power the game has ever seen, Mickey Mantle captured the imagination of a generation. A three-time Most Valuable Player, Mantle won the Triple Crown in 1956. Despite being plagued by injuries, he hit over .300 ten times and played in 12 World Series for a team that won seven World Championships during his career.

Photo courtesy: Steiner Sports.

doing. Before he began speaking or signing autographs, he would ask what was expected of him. When he was done, he always asked if there was anything more he could do. Mantle was often willing to take less money for a personal appearance if his teammates could be included and make a few bucks.

I was too young to see Mantle play for the New York Yankees. In the 1950s and early 1960s, he was still at his peak as a player. But I've heard the stories of how great he was, and, after appearing with him, I understood why his teammates held him in such esteem. On his plaque in "Monument Park"—a kind of open-air museum of plaques beyond the Stadium's leftfield fence in tribute to dozens of great Yankees from Babe Ruth to the present—a line reads, "Mickey Mantle, a Great Teammate." After winning the Triple Crown in 1956—a rarity since a player must lead the league in home runs, runs batted in, and batting average— Mickey was making $65,000 a year, which sounds paltry in light of today's salaries. But you have to remember that his teammates—Moose Skowron, Gil McDougal, Hank Bauer, Tony Kubek, and many others— were only making a fraction of that. A salary of $10,000 was considered very good at that time.

When Mickey was injured, his teammates were eager for him to get healthy, partly because they knew they had a much better chance of winning the World Series with him. If they won the Series, they would get a Series share of about $8,000 and double their salaries for a week's work. For all the time Mantle was injured, he missed only one Series, which was in 1961. He played just one game in that one, but the team won easily without him.

Mickey Mantle never thought he deserved all the fuss. He really didn't understand what it was all about. He retired with 536 home runs, which at that time was behind only Babe Ruth and Willie Mays. But those who knew him knew he deserved "the fuss" not only because of his achievements, but also because of his humble attitude.

Unfortunately, there are sports celebrities who don't even come close to Mickey's reputation, but who have an attitude that says, "I'm a star and you're not—you should be lucky I even showed up."

Fortunately, the woods are full of people who give everything they have to give. I have worked with NBA coach Pat Riley and would definitely work with him again. Steiner Sports had booked Pat for a speaking engagement for a major sporting goods chain. You must understand that when we book speakers for corporate events, we usually send them a single page of background information on the company. Pat sent *us* a five-page questionnaire about the company. That's pretty unusual, to say the least. After we finished filling out the five pages, he called back and asked us to do specific research on the sporting goods industry. He had at least ten in-depth questions about the industry.

I couldn't believe it. I could see then how this guy from Schenectady, New York, had lasted nine years as a player in the NBA and is regarder as one of the two or three greatest coaches ever. It's because of what is inside of him. Riley taught me something right then and there about leaving no stone unturned. We did the research he asked for, well in advance of his appearance. Now you may have heard that Pat Riley is one excellent speaker. By the time he finished his speech, people were standing on the tables! That's how hyped those people were: standing ovation, on the chairs, on the tables! That's how on-the-money he was with his talk to those 200 people. Riley is tall, handsome, well-spoken, and altogether charismatic to begin with, but he didn't stop at that—he took the time to get the background information, did all the preparation, and knew how to speak the language of his audience.

I learned firsthand that baseball Hall of Famer Phil Rizzuto is another guy who's big on going the extra mile. He still corresponds with fans—he's in touch with several hundred fans on a regular basis. And he will always go out of his way for them. One day, we were in Yankee

NOT GOING EVEN A HALF-MILE

L en Dykstra was one of those celebrities. Dykstra played for the Mets and the Phillies in the '80s and '90s. When he was with the Phillies, he did an appearance for Steiner Sports in New Jersey. Now, I had been trying to do business with the marketing vice president of Nobody Beats the Wiz, a wildly successful appliance chain, for a year and a half. The firm was doing a ton of athlete appearances at that time, and I tried to hook up with them but hadn't gotten a call back no matter how many calls I had tried. Well, finally I got hold of him and would have my chance to impress him and get his ongoing business.

The appearance would be at a Cherry Hill, New Jersey, Wiz store. Because of the location, I thought Dykstra would be perfect since it was between Philadelphia and New York so Mets and Phillies fans could come. I had Dykstra picked up in a car, and from the moment he got in, he was on the phone. Car phone charges then were $.75 a minute, and he ran up a bill of more than $1,000. The plan was to have him sign some autographs at the store. Sure enough, more than 1,000 fans were lined up to meet Dykstra. After being a half hour late, Dykstra was nasty to all of them. The night game he was playing in after the signing had turned into a two-night double-header due to a previous rainout, and he told me the Wiz was lucky he showed up at all. He threatened to leave early, and I had to hide the car so he couldn't. While Dykstra carried on in this disgraceful way, the marketing vice president was standing next to me. Needless to say, he was livid that this spoiled athlete was ruining a Wiz promotion. Steiner Sports never got to work with the Wiz again. I wrote it off as a singular nightmare and vowed never to work with Dykstra again.

Two of the great Yankees of all time. Phil Rizzuto and Derek Jeter are the two most important players I have had the pleasure of knowing. Both are two great shortstops. You should never stop short (short stop, get it?) of your dreams. These two guys have been a dream come true to be associated with.

Photo courtesy: Steiner Sports.

Stadium after making a couple of appearances there for some of the corporate sponsors we deal with. I was trying to take Phil through the details of a rather large deal, but he ran into a group of fans. They were just regular guys; one had a construction hat on, but I had to wait 20 minutes in the middle of discussing a $100,000 deal because Phil was talking about some of the best places to get cannoli in Brooklyn! One of these guys had been one of Phil's fans since the 1950s, and had seen Phil play when he was a little kid. When I asked Phil about the incident, he said, "Brandon, the money's great, but I live and die for talking to these people." He always gives everyone that kind of respect.

Then there was the night we were having dinner at Yankee Stadium with a group of top salesmen. They had won a prize—tickets to a Yankee game and a dinner with Phil, their company's spokesman, beforehand. So one of the guys at the table said, "Phil, I'd really like to get a photo for my nephew who's ill. He wasn't able to come because he's in the hospital." And Phil said, "Give me his phone number." And right there, on his own cell phone, he talked to the kid for 15 minutes, a call that was not cheap at the time. It was phenomenal. Phil has never lost his sensitivity and always goes the extra mile.

UNDERPROMISE AND OVERDELIVER

All you have to do to go the extra mile is underpromise and overdeliver. Make it one of your habits in all of your dealings with people. I know it seems difficult in business where so many things are contracted, written, and signed—or "carved in stone" as they say. In a world of line items and tight negotiations it's not easy to give more without determining immediately what the return will be. Do it anyway. The return will come; not always when you want it, not always from the expected place, but here again, if you give good, you'll get good. What goes around *really does* come around.

Leaders who go the extra mile can usually count on others to do the same. Talking about former teammate Mark Messier, retired New York Ranger Nick Kypreos told me, "You can't put a dollar value on making people feel comfortable, you can't equate money with developing trust or building a family type of relationship. Mess is the kind of guy who has true leadership that way, doing the things that don't show up in the box scores." Nick was talking about the kind of leadership that encourages others to give their best as well.

Mark always spends time with the families of new players, making them feel comfortable in new surroundings. He rented a bus for the Ranger team wives so they could travel together to New York City, have lunch, shop, and get to know each other. That's a little of what Nick meant about building family relationships. On one occasion, a new player came up; young and broke. Like a lot of young athletes beginning a professional career, the new guy didn't even own a suit. Messier, a leader, knowing that the team would have to dress up for certain events, took matters into his own hands. The next day, hanging on the young player's locker, was a brand new suit with a note that read, "Welcome to the NHL!"

When his team faced elimination in game six of the conference finals against the New Jersey Devils in 1994, and Messier made a public prediction guaranteeing victory. Don't you think his teammates reached down deep to give him all they had on the ice? They summoned all their effort, and it helped the Rangers win the Stanley Cup.

If the guys who don't have to do it can go the extra mile, we can, too.

You'll need to plan how and when to go the extra mile while you're building the habit, until it becomes second nature. When you're in a negotiating situation—and remember we're in negotiating situations all day long, with everyone—be mentally willing to give more than whatever is stated, more than "what's on the page." It isn't necessary at this point to let the other person know what you're willing to give, of course, but you need to know that you're going to pleasantly surprise him or her.

Make sure that in your negotiations, you leave yourself room to overdeliver. You do this by *underpromising*. It's so easy to overpromise, to offer the moon, to lowball a bid; but restrain yourself. Be able to keep your word and more. You build a reputation with each and every promise you make.

Decide how far the extra mile is right at the beginning. While you're still at the point of negotiation, assess what you're giving in the deal, and how much more you'll give, *or you won't do it.* This is crucial. Make the decision for yourself as early as possible. A good rule of thumb is to always give yourself an extra one-third margin. This allows you room for error, and if there's no error, you get to delight your customer.

You'll need to trust your instincts as to when to "deliver the over," but generally sooner is better than later. It gratifies the other person to know that you're taking care of his or her needs and more. It also makes the person feel more secure in dealing with you, and if you can, help the other person feel they've gotten the better part of any negotiation. Then you're really making them feel good!

GO THE EXTRA MILE, BUT DON'T
DO IT WALKING ON YOUR HANDS

If you're overly excessive in what you're giving up, you may produce the opposite effect from the one you intended. Think about how you feel when someone is just too accommodating: Doesn't it send up a red flag? Again, you'll need to trust your instincts here, but if you put yourself in the other person's position and give what you'd like to get, you'll be fine.

One more thing is important here. It's all right to point out—once and only once—that you've given the other person more than you promised, that you've taken care of them.

KEEP INCREASING YOUR CAPACITY

At any given time, most of us think we're doing as much work as we can. An employee came to me recently and said, "Brandon, I am swamped. I can't possibly take on another thing!" I asked, "Are you doing more than you were a year ago?" The answer, of course, was yes. But a year before, the same employee had said he was swamped and couldn't take on another thing. Each of us sets our own ground rules regarding what our capacity really is, and we increase it one step at a time.

A marathon runner didn't start out running marathons. Like a runner who adds miles gradually, we stretch our capacity through practice and learning how to manage our time and energy. No one knows for sure what his or her limits are, but we constantly put limits on ourselves. I won't say that we create roadblocks for ourselves, but we certainly put our own tollbooths on the bridges we need to cross.

When I started Steiner Sports, I thought that if the firm could just get to the point where it could book celebrities for ten appearances a month, it would be in great shape. That was the goal. It looked big—ten appearances with celebrity athletes every month! Today we do approximately 150 appearances a month! If someone had asked me back then if I thought we'd ever be able to do 150 appearances a month, I'd have said the idea was insane.

I've read a lot of books that talk about an imaginary line that people stop themselves from crossing—stories about salesmen who slow down when they approach their quota. People seem to keep track, consciously or unconsciously, of how much they give to their employers. Maybe they don't realize that when they hold back, they hold themselves back.

Pat Riley talks about players who put it all on the table, who hold nothing back. Pat says he doesn't want a player who holds back—that it affects the team like a clot in a vein. A player who doesn't give his or her all creates an unhealthy backup in a team.

One of the most important ways to really stretch your capacity and give your best is to learn to manage your priorities better. That may require a change in how you think about time.

TIME MANAGEMENT IS REALLY PRIORITY MANAGEMENT

When you say you don't have time, it's simply not true! Every one of us has the same 24 hours every day. When you don't have time for something, it means something else was more important.

You need to be realistic about how you spend your time. Allow yourself a certain amount of goofing-off time, but be aware of it! You're going to take that time anyway. Here's what I mean. Let's say you're working eight hours a day—480 minutes a day. Do you think you do 480 minutes of solid work? Of course not. There's ten minutes on this conversation, another ten minutes on that. Now, if you're conscious of your time, you can take control of it. One conversation can be cut by three minutes, another one is going on five minutes too long—that's eight minutes, and that's just in one hour!

You need to look at your time like a talk-radio station looks at time. A station has 42 minutes of talk and 18 minutes of commercials. Now you can't work 60 minutes out of every hour—it's not realistic. But you have to make a commitment to how many minutes you're going to work each hour. You have phone calls, diversions, conversations. You need to allow yourself to say, "Excuse me, please come back at 12." Sometimes you have to say no to interruptions, once you've reached your self-imposed time limit.

We all get the same 24 hours every day, and I don't think it's possible for any of us to conceive of all the things we could possibly do with our time. I think you just have to be open to the possibilities. Very often we adhere to rules that aren't there, such as "I don't work weekends" or "I don't want to work late." That makes sense to me if you've got something to do, or if you're going to spend time with your family, but what I tell my employees is, "If you're going to go home and do nothing, you might as well do nothing here!" If there's something unfinished at work that's going to be preying on your mind, why not stay late or come in on a Saturday so you can have a clear head about it the next day? Why go home and worry about all you've got to do the next day?

Now, if you're regularly overwhelmed, if you find yourself needing to work late or on weekends on a regular basis, then you need to sit down with your supervisor (or yourself if you're self-employed) and make some changes; that's not balanced or healthy. But to catch up from time to time, to do it occasionally instead of sitting in front of the TV, will benefit you in the long run. The best executives, the best managers, the best workers at any level are the ones who find their own time. I know a number of people who start their workday at 5 A.M. twice a week just to give themselves those extra hours before anyone else comes in, before the phones ring and the interruptions begin, to clear away the backup, to deal with the minutiae. Some people come in one Saturday a month to do the same. I have yet to meet a rising, successful person who hasn't come in very early or stayed late on occasion—not just for emergencies. Finding your own time, privately, to organize yourself is a key to increasing your capacity.

Increasing Your Capacity in Legendary Fashion

At 5 feet 7 inches and 118 pounds in high school, Ozzie Smith wasn't about to overwhelm baseball scouts with his physical stature. If he wanted to play Major League Baseball, it would be the size of his heart that would come into play.

Smith had a scholarship to California Polytechnic and proceeded to school himself in hitting left-handed. But he was homesick and went back to St. Louis. From there, Smith joined a pro team in Clarinda, Iowa. Manager Merle Eberle took one look and said, "He looked too damned small to pick up a bat." But what got Eberle's attention was Smith's attitude. As Eberle pounded ball after ball his way at shortstop, Smith finally said, "Mr. Eberle, don't you know you can't get one by me?"

Smith led Clarinda to a national tournament, then returned to Cal Poly, and was snatched up by the San Diego Padres in the 1977 draft. After seeing Smith, Padres' manager Alvin Dark declared, "I have my shortstop." The move didn't sit well with management, since Bill Almond was already under contract at that position and Dark wouldn't survive his unpopular move. Before departing, Dark said

Photo courtesy: Steiner Sports.

to Ozzie,"Don't change a thing." "Alvin Dark got fired for bringing a 130-pound shortstop to the bigs," said Ozzie. But in a short period of time, another former infielder would confirm Dark's judgment: "He is the most acrobatic shortstop ever," said Jerry Coleman, broadcaster and former Yankee second baseman.

In his rookie season, Smith made what many baseball fans consider the greatest defensive play ever made. He dove for a hot shot up the middle, but the ball hit a pebble, and instead of heading for his glove hand, bounced back into his body. Fully extended, Smith reached back with his bare hand, grabbed it, got to his feet, and threw the runner out.

By 1980, Smith had set the assists record for shortstops and earned his first of 13 Gold Gloves. Playing in back of Ozzie in leftfield, future Hall of Famer Dave Winfield saw it all unfold. "He caught everything on the ground," Winfield remembers. "I knew that I had to put the time in if I wanted to be a better player, defensively, offensively," Ozzie says. "I've heard people say, 'I leave my work at the office.' Anyone who is great at what they do doesn't leave their work at the office."

Smith's goal was to make each season better than the last. Look at his career statistics, and you can't help but notice how his batting average and on-base percentage increased as the years went by. "I had to learn not to hit under the ball, since I didn't have the power," he explains. "I practiced hitting down on the ball." The results were more line drives and hard grounders that found holes in the infield, instead of weak pop flies that found gloves. "He was never satisfied with the type of hitter he was and made himself better," said Tony Gwynn, himself an eight-time batting champion who began his career with the Padres in 1984.

But Smith had problems with the management in San Diego, and manager Whitey Herzog wanted him in St. Louis. He helped the Cardinals win the

World Series in 1982 and make it back to the Series in 1985 and 1987. After the 1982 Series, Smith signed a three-year deal that made him baseball's first $1 million shortstop.

After 15 All-Star seasons, Smith retired in 1996 and was voted to the baseball Hall of Fame in 2001, his first season of eligibility.

IF YOU'RE CHALLENGING YOURSELF, TIME ISN'T AN ISSUE

We can all ask, "How much time do I need to work a week to be successful?" In my experience, there's only one correct answer—whatever time it takes. If you're answering that question in hours, then you need to reevaluate what it is you want. If I can get my work done, have some fun, make some money, and spend some time with my family, I've had a very successful day. I have no idea how many hours I put in! It's vital to keep the balance, but you can't be entrepreneurial and stare at your watch at the same time.

If you tell yourself that if you work more than 40 hours in a week you're going to be exhausted, you probably will be. But I'm sure that if you think about it, you've put out Herculean efforts and spent enormous amounts of time on projects that you enjoyed or that were important to you.

Readers who know my story know some of the things I've done. When I was six, back in 1965, I started going away to Camp Sussex in Sussex, New Jersey, with my friends. It was a great relief for a kid like me to get out of the sweltering heat of Brooklyn for three weeks every summer. I ended up going to summer camp every summer until I was 15 and then I worked in the kitchen there for six more years, through the end of college.

I learned some really valuable lessons when I started working there. I started as a waiter, then washed dishes, and rose to the level of second chef for Alzie Jackson. Many people wouldn't want that job. For a nine-week summer with one day off I worked in the kitchen—13-hour days with a two-hour break—where the temperature was more than 100 degrees. It was unbelievably taxing physically, and we never felt better in our lives. We knew what the job required, and we were trained to do it. We knew were doing a good thing—working for some 500 kids, the same kinds of kids from poor, broken homes that we had been in years before. For me it was the beginning of the attitude that carried me into the restaurant business and the work ethic that carried me further.

People who love and enjoy what they're doing are constantly pushing ahead—not just for their company, but also for themselves. Who's looking at the clock? This may sound harsh, but if you're clockwatching, you might consider throwing that watch away and getting another job! There are jobs for clockwatchers, and I've got nothing against them, but there's no timepiece over the door to success.

Another way to keep increasing your capacity is to keep asking yourself, "What else?" Ask yourself at least six times a day. If you're not asking "what else," you're not on the increase. With Ozzie Smith, the goal was to have a better year than the year before. Now, did that mean one more stolen base, one more assist, one more whatever? Smith said, "The performance of the year before predicted what you would have to do the next year."

Don't just ask yourself, either! Ask your customers, "What else do you need?" Ask your family, friends, coworkers, "How else can I help?" Jared Weiss (my V.P. remember?) closes many conversations with, "What else?"

COVER THE BASICS

One part of going the extra mile is covering the basics. Too many people overlook basics, sometimes referred to as "the little things." But little things add up to be enormously important.

Frank Borman, past president of Eastern Airlines, once said, "If our ashtrays are dirty, people think we're not maintaining our engines." Borman was saying that even the little things can cost us our reputation.

Sometimes we need to remind ourselves of the basics. Football hero Joe Namath told me a story about his days at the University of Alabama. One day, the team was warming up in a practice session. Joe didn't look like he was throwing the ball in rhythm that day, so coach Bear Bryant walked over to him and said, "Look, Joe, you take the football, and you hold it like this, and—ah, what am I telling you for, you know more about this than I do." Then he threw the football back to him and walked away. The point was just to get Namath back to the basics. They say NFL legendary coach Vince Lombardi began every training session by holding up the pigskin and saying, "Gentlemen, this is a football." Because most of us don't have a coach physically guiding our steps, we need to be able to remind ourselves of the basics and what they are for us.

Gordie Howe is known as "Mr. Hockey." He started playing professional hockey with the Saskatoon Lions in 1943, played 25 years with the Detroit Red Wings, and at the age of 52 played 80 games with the Hartford Whalers in 1980. Then

Gordie Howe was one of the greatest hockey players in NHL history. Gordie starred for the Detroit Red Wings and played in seven different decades. He is second all-time in goals scored.

Photo courtesy: Getty Images.

he returned, at age 70, to play a game for the Detroit Vipers. He told me his basics were self-denial, hard work, and a good diet.

If I wasn't skating as well as I thought I could, I'd go out and skate a little extra after practice, maybe an hour more. To get the proper sleep, you have to sacrifice something—you sacrifice what you eat and the hours you keep. When Colleen and I got married at a young age, she cooked what was good for me, not necessarily what I enjoyed.

The little things, the details, are the things that may be taken for granted, even go unnoticed—until you leave them out. When I come home from the office or a business trip, in fact, whenever I walk in the door, I kiss my wife hello. Now she doesn't usually thank me for the kiss, and no brass band plays "76 Trombones" from *The Music Man*. I'd hate to think she didn't notice, but that's possible, too. But I KNOW she'd notice if I came into the house and DIDN'T give her a kiss! Try not complimenting your wife or girlfriend after she spends $150 on a hairdo, and you will come face to face with what happens when you overlook the basics—the hard way.

EVERY ONE OF US IS IN OUR OWN SERVICE BUSINESS

Working on an assembly line means serving the end-user, serving your foreman, and serving everyone else up and down the line. One of the basics is a shift in your attitude. You're always in your own business, you're always serving customers, and paying attention to the little things that make your customer happy is the key to being a champion.

I like to use restaurants as an example, because I come from the restaurant business. A food server who wants to increase his or her tips always has the basics covered. The customer's water glass is always filled, the waiter always has at least $1 in change at all times (you never know when your customer needs to use the pay phone!), and if you're waiting tables in the smoking section, you carry a lighter. These things are so simple, so basic, but they create an atmosphere of ease for the customer and an air of competence and service in the waiter.

But, you say, I'm not a waiter! I'm a secretary, or a salesperson, or a product manager, or a corporate vice president, or a sanitation worker, or a librarian. It doesn't matter what you do! You're in a service business. The fact is, you are in your own service business, and when you start looking at your work in that context, it becomes easier to understand the basics. A simple attitude adjustment can make a world of difference. Look at how most of us regard our jobs: "I'm trading my hours for dollars. My boss tells me what he or she wants, and I do it. Then I go home and live what's left of my life."

That sounds too much like work to me. Try this shift in attitude. "I'm in my own business, and I've contracted with (the company you work for) to give them the best service I can render in exchange for an agreed-upon compensation package. He/she is not my boss, but my customer." The work may be the same, but this kind of attitude puts you in control of the situation and makes you the boss of your business. It's an attitude that will earn you more money and less stress in the long run.

Now here's the hard news: Although the rewards are much sweeter, being the boss means working harder and smarter than ever. As the boss of my business, I've learned that I'm the ultimate servant. I've got people who work for me, sure, and they work damned hard, but I work for everyone. I've got to satisfy my clients, my prospective clients, my employees, and the guy who delivers my Danish and coffee in the morning. I've got to serve almost everyone I meet in some way, large or small. And, if you want to be successful, so do you.

Whether or not you've got people who report to you, look for the little things you can do to help the people around you. Help by listening attentively to them, understanding their needs and motivations, and teaching them the things you know. The people you serve in these ways will be ready and willing to help you when you need it—and the time always comes when you will.

Return phone calls on time. If someone e-mails in the morning or midday, get back to the person by the end of the day. It is called e-mail, after all, not the Pony Express; so don't keep correspondents waiting. If it takes more than a day, what is your response worth? It may be too late to offer the assistance they requested. It's simple consideration.

I have a friend who interviews many athletes. He knows the difference between the guys who are genuinely nice and the ones who are only kind to people when a camera is on. He told me that Major League clubhouses are full of people who are intolerably surly and only change their attitude when an ESPN camera crew or the sports anchor for the evening news comes along. He interviewed Terry Bradshaw, former Pittsburgh Steelers star and now TV broadcaster, for a major magazine. Bradshaw not only spent four hours with him for the interview, but he picked up the check for lunch! Now, Terry may turn in the receipt to his employer, and my friend's magazine would have picked up the expense if he hadn't.

Photo courtesy: Getty Images.

Wayne Gretzky, the peerless #99 and always one of the most gracious interviews in sports.

But it doesn't matter: It was the kindness of the gesture, as if he was saying, "I've enjoyed this, too; please let me pay this."

Wayne Gretzky, hockey's "Great One," was equally as gracious, sitting hours for the interview and inviting the writer back to his sports restaurant in New York to hang out for the photo shoot. Former NFL coach Mike Ditka can be pretty gruff with reporters, but he too picked up the check and spent hours taking the writer around New Orleans, to a cigar bar and an expensive restaurant in the French Quarter. He's just a genuine guy. Red Auerbach, as is his custom ever since his Celtic coaching days in the 1950s, takes writers to Chinese restaurants, where they talk. If he sees the writer the next day, he asks "Do you need anything else?" Now, what do all of these people have in common? In case you haven't noticed, they're all in the Hall of Fame for their sports. And if people that "important" can afford to be giving and take time, then why can't we all?

I'm not saying that you should be so full of kindness in your day-to-day activities that you allow doing favors to fill your day. And you can't allow a series of distractions—be they phone calls or e-mails or office conversations—to rule your day. Someone near and dear to me once said, "If you're always thinking about little things, you will become a little thing." He meant that we must have larger plans and stick to them to achieve our goals. You must run your clock, or else you'll find circumstances—and others—running it for you.

"Iron" Mike Ditka, giving an official an earful.

Photo courtesy: Getty Images.

DON'T GIVE IN TO THE "TYRANNY OF THE IMMEDIATE"

Many people are so consumed with five-minute tasks, that by the time two o'clock rolls around, they haven't gotten to their day's work. All they've done is handle a series of minor distractions and douse brush fires. Now add those days to other days, and to weeks and to months and to years, and that is all some people have achieved by the end of their lives. It is frightful but true.

Each of us has to separate *urgent* tasks from *important* ones. If you don't, you will be forever neglectful of what is important—what is important will get buried by some urgent task or another.

But within the framework of your goal-oriented behavior, you must be able to accept some deviations. If little kindnesses and favors are called for, and time is of the essence for fulfilling those favors, then you ought to do them. It's good for building personal relationships and—what amounts to the same thing—it's good business. These matters are basic but inestimably important.

A champion doesn't coast; there's no automatic pilot. But keeping it simple and covering the basics will make the life of a champion doable and very enjoyable for you.

Former Dallas Cowboys quarterback Roger Staubach once told me, "Success in business is the same as in football; having your priorities right, doing the little things. Not only meeting the expectations that your customer has, but exceeding those expectations."

Learn, practice, and do the simple, basic things that lead to living the life of a champion—for success in work and every other area of your life.

—— *Chapter Review* ——

▸ Decide at the outset how long the extra mile is; what you're willing to give.

▶ Consider the timing of the extra mile (sooner is better than later).

▶ No matter how good your intentions, being excessive in what you're giving will send up a "red flag."

▶ Increase your capacity through practice and time management.

▶ Organize yourself at least once a week.

▶ There's no timepiece over the door to success.

▶ Keep doing the simple, basic things. It's more important to get on base regularly than to hit the long ball.

▶ Pay attention to the details. They only go unnoticed until you leave them out.

▶ See yourself as being in your own service business, and see everyone else as your customer.

▶ Make the people you work for your best customers.

▶ Don't give in to the "tyranny of the immediate."

▶ Deviate from your plans to fulfill simple favors.

Walter Payton, running here at Soldier Field, ran past Jimmie Brown's 12,312-yard NFL-record. In 1987, Payton finished his 13-year career with 3,838 carries and 16,726 yards.

An optimist sees an opportunity in every calamity;

a pessimist sees a calamity in every opportunity

—Anonymous.

YOU NEVER KNOW

The title of this chapter is one of my favorite sayings. Unfortunately, the New York Lottery people started using, "Hey, you never know" in promotional campaigns before I could copyright the phrase. But I still use it, and "you never know" is still at the core of my philosophy.

When I sat down at my secondhand, ink-stained metal desk with a phone, a card file, and my minimal investment in Steiner Sports, I didn't know it would become the success it is today. I hoped, I planned, I worked, I visualized. But I didn't know. I took chances, I played the percentages, and sometimes I was wrong and took a financial bath. But you never know. You never know who you're dealing with, what someone can do for you, what someone can add to your life or your future, so always treat everyone like gold, because they might be great assets. You never know.

When I was working at the Hard Rock Cafe in New York City, the place was a happening spot. Different kinds of people came in representing every occupation, every path of life—from the barber next door to the CEOs from all over the city to the out-of-town kids. I worked hard to treat each and every one of them as a special person, a special customer. The rest of the staff would fawn over the rock stars to the point where it was embarrassing, and some of the staff would be nice to the tourists. I began to notice that the professional athletes who visited were not exactly ignored, but not treated with the kind of respect I thought they deserved.

So I made certain to give the athletes special treatment. I had no way of knowing then that working with some of these men would be how I make my living today; I just wanted to make sure they were treated properly. They never forgot it. I didn't know then, but you never know.

Everyone talks about the 80–20 principle: 80 percent of your business comes from 20 percent of your clients; 80 percent of the conflicts in your life come from 20 percent of the people you know; 80 percent of your files are rarely used—there are examples everywhere. In 1999 Steiner Sports did about 250 deals, maybe more—but most of our income was generated by *three deals!* The problem with applying the 80–20 rule is that *you never know* where it's going to apply. No one is clairvoyant. Going in, does anyone know which 20 percent of their contacts are going to be beneficial?

At Steiner we didn't know which deals would be the big ones, but the signings of Derek Jeter, Mia Hamm, and Walter Payton turned out to be huge. We didn't know we'd be able to sign those athletes, but they made our year.

My relationship with the late Walter Payton began in 1993. Walter, the superstar Chicago Bear, had always seen himself as a servant, endlessly doing his best to please the public. He viewed himself as public domain, so even though I'd been bugging Walter since 1993 to do collectibles, to do a licensing deal, something—he always said no. But in February 1999, I got a phone call. Walter was ill and had decided the time was right to produce a collectible, and he chose to work with Steiner Sports. He died in November 1999. Looking back now, I think he was beginning to face his own mortality even before he called us and wanted a greater degree of control over his legacy. That legacy included being the all-time NFL rusher with 16,726 yards, until Emmitt Smith passed that mark (but with fewer yards per carry) in 2002. If you can't remember Payton's yard total, just try to think of it as being slightly under ten miles.

Besides his football legacy, which was impeccable, Walter was such a giving person that I believe he wanted to leave as much of himself to as many people as possible, and also to continue to do his best to take care of his loved ones.

He chose Steiner Sports because he had a relationship with us and had trust in us. Eventually, treating people right comes back to you. You never know. The fundamental here is: You can never stop putting your best foot forward, you can never stop doing the right thing, because *you never know* who's watching.

YOU NEVER KNOW WHERE YOU MIGHT WIND UP

Gary Carter just got his Cooperstown credentials in August 2003. His climb to success very definitely has a "you never know" quality. For those of you who don't remember, Gary Carter was the best catcher in baseball for more than a decade, from the mid-1970s to the mid-1980s. His career took off early. He won the All-Star Game MVP in 1981 and again in 1984. He had signed a seven-year extension with the Expos in 1982, so he figured to be a mainstay in Montreal. Then it happened.

The moment of victory! Gary Carter celebrating the New York Mets' Game 7 victory in the 1986 World Series.

Photo courtesy: Getty Images.

My biggest surprise was when the Expos traded me. I thought I was going to be an Expo for my entire career! I didn't see it coming at all; it's something I didn't expect. I had just come off my best year with the Expos, driving in 106 runs, hitting .294, something like that, and had 27 homers. And it floored me to think the front office wanted to trade me. We had finished in fifth place, so that might have had something to do with it. But I thought I was locked in.

The only thing helping me out was the five and ten rule. If you have five years with the same team and ten years total, you have the right to veto any trade. That's what I had at the end of the 1984 season. I didn't want to go just anywhere. There were only three teams I wanted to go to—the Dodgers, Braves, and Mets. There was almost a deal to Atlanta and then that fell through, so that was the best thing that ever happened to me.

It was the best thing that ever happened because he went to the Mets, and in his second year there, the team won the World Series. Here he was floored, leaving a city he loved. But it turned out that better experiences lay ahead. Carter had always wanted to play in a World Series. At the age of 32, he did.

YOU NEVER KNOW ABOUT
INVOLUNTARY COMMITMENT

Another aspect of "you never know" is what I call "involuntary commitment." Involuntary commitment is putting yourself in situations where you *must* perform, even if you're in deeper than you had planned.

The best example of involuntary commitment that I've ever heard is a story that legendary football coach Lou Holtz tells:

> There was a fire in a small town that had been burning for days, and everyone in town had been trying to put it out every way possible, but the fire was burning too hot for the firemen to get close. All the townspeople are watching the buildings burn, when the richest man in town offers $100,000 to anyone who can put out the fire. Suddenly, a tiny pumper engine comes barreling down the street, siren blaring, horns honking, straight into the flaming jaws of the fire! Within an hour, the flames are down, and a lone firefighter comes out from among the smoldering ashes.

The rich man came forward to shake the fireman's hand and give him the check for the $100,000. He asked the sooty hero, "What will you do with the money?"

"Well," said the fireman, "*First*, I'm gonna get the brakes fixed on my truck!"

YOU NEVER KNOW WHERE
YOUR CAREER WILL TAKE YOU

One of the best "you never know" stories happened to my friend, Bill Walton. Bill was a basketball machine, a Hall of Famer who over a decade battled 30 operations to his feet because of stress fractures. He had one of the greatest talent quotients of anyone who ever played the game. But he had a problem for a long time that he rarely talked about.

He had a terrible speech impediment, so much so that he dreaded getting in front of people to speak.

"During college, the teasing was tough," he told me. "I had a speech class one year, and they laughed me out of the class." It didn't matter to his classmates that he was the College Basketball Player of the Year. "I was trying to make it in school, and they just laughed me out of the class." It was more than a minor hindrance. He often struggled to get out a complete sentence without that stammering, halting interruption to his thought.

On the court, he could be as verbal as he needed to be. He could speak and yell, when it was called for. "I never had any trouble yelling at the refs," Walton said. "In the heat of the game . . . when it was just totally spontaneous, I could get out there and really scream and yell at the refs. But it was only in basketball, and it was only at the refs."

Walton credited the late Marty Glickman, a broadcaster and Olympic sprinter in the 1936 Olympics, with helping him overcome his stuttering. Walton said Glickman pulled him aside at a social gathering when Walton was 28 and gave him instructions on how to overcome his stuttering and use various drills to develop his speech skills. "Learning how to speak has given me a whole new life," Walton said. "I have been set free."

Walton now works as a broadcaster, calling college and professional basketball games for TV networks. About the speech problem, he says, "Obviously, I still have problems with it, and I will always have problems with it. The most difficult part is the waiting, the anticipation— almost the same feeling you get when you are playing. All the elements that I loved as a player are there in my new job. You have to be calm, restrained, disciplined, and those are not things that come easily to me. But for me to make my living as a broadcaster and a public speaker— who would have ever thought it? That is the most unlikely career path for me."

A Personal "You Never Know"

I lived through my own "you never know" tale. When I graduated Syracuse University—with a B.S. in accounting and personal industrial relations—I went on an interview in a suburb of Baltimore, for a job managing a hospital cafeteria. Hospital officials liked me, and the job seemed like a pretty good deal. They even offered to "put me up for 90 days until I got my own place." They said they knew of a trailer in a trailer park only "a couple of miles" from the hospital. I took the job and drove down from Brooklyn with $600 and two suits. When I went for the interview I hadn't seen the distance of my trailer from my job.

In reality, the trailer park turned out to be 30 miles away from the hospital, in the town of East Nowhere, north of Lost in Space. I was the youngest person in the park by 40 years. So this Brooklyn guy found himself knowing no one in a place where I had to drive miles to a store to buy milk and bread. I was lost in a strange world. Strange place, strange conditions, and even the attractive nurses had suddenly disappeared!

I told anyone who would listen that I needed to make a change. I told my mother that I wanted to come home. Instead of agreeing to have me come back, she gave me a phone number of someone she knew I could stay with. I didn't want to make the call. After all, how can a 22-year-old be cool and take advice from his mother at the same time? For the next few months, I bounced from one bad living situation to another. Finally, I took my mother's advice and called Joel, who is the son of my mother's friend, Sarah. Joel offered me a room in his basement. Out of desperation, I took it. I wasn't exactly living the high life, and I didn't really see my way forward.

About a month later, I mentioned to Joel and his wife Susan that I wanted to work in the hotel business. He said, "Did you know there's a big Hyatt downtown?" I didn't even know how to get downtown! He drove me there, and I got the last open management position at the Grand Hyatt in Baltimore.

At the orientation, I met two of the younger executives, Tom Pagel and Rich Cortese, at Hyatt who shared a house and were looking for a third room-mate! One thing led to another, and Hyatt put me on my way. From hotel management, I got into restaurant management, which is how I met ath-letes and got going with Steiner Sports.

BUT YOU MIGHT HAVE A HUNCH

Sometimes you never know, but you might suspect. Those are the times when you've got to go with your hunches. I was on the phone with New York Giants running back Ottis Anderson when he was in San Francisco in 1990, preparing for the NFC championship game. Ottis and I had done some promotions together in 1986, when he hadn't been one of the Giants' big names. His Rookie-of-the-Year season was way behind him already. And in '90, nobody thought the Giants were going to beat the San Francisco '49ers—especially on the road. I said, "Ottis, you're definitely winning this game, and when you go to the Super Bowl, since you'll be the running back of the winning team, you're going to be the MVP. After you smile for the camera and say, 'I'm going to Disney World,' I want you to know that I want to handle everything for you."

I think Ottis was taken aback—I don't think he'd considered the possibility of being the Super Bowl MVP. Of course, the Giants won that game with the '49ers, and Ottis called me back. "You know something?" he said. "I had a dream the other night that I really am gonna win the MVP!" He did win it, running for more than 100 yards against Buffalo in Super Bowl XXV. And after the Giants' Super Bowl win over the Bills, we were on a promotions run together, and I was Ottis's guy. We both had the time of our lives, and we both made money.

Give everyone the red carpet treatment. You never know.

YOU NEVER KNOW ABOUT NO

Part of "you never know" is that sometimes when people tell you no, what they really mean is yes. Especially when people give a really quick, abrupt no, what they really mean is "I don't understand; break it down for me. Take me through it." What you need to do with those kinds of "no" is to find out what it is they're saying no to.

Recognize that "no" is sometimes an unconscious request for more information. Discover the other person's objections, uncover his or her concerns and address them. Take the time to do this instead of giving up. Let me give you an example of how this works.

For a time, Steiner Sports was doing some work with the Yoo-Hoo company. Yoo-Hoo is a chocolate milk drink and Yankee Hall of Famer Yogi Berra and Yoo-Hoo were synonymous in the 1950s and 1960s. Berra first met the Olivieris, the founders of the popular drink, at a New Jersey country club in 1955. Berra liked the drink and in no time he was endors-

ing it in appearances and advertisements. Whitey Ford, his teammate and a future Hall of Famer, joined him in advertisements. Yogi and

Phil Rizzuto (left) and Yogi Berra are both Yankee Hall of Famers and both did promotional work for Yoo-Hoo in the '90s.

Photo courtesy: Getty Images.

Kirk Gibson of the Los Angeles Dodgers rounds the bases in celebration after hitting a game winning, pinch-hit homerun in the bottom of the ninth against the Oakland athletics during Game One of the 1988 World Series in Los Angeles. Gibson's blow turned the entire series in the Dodgers' favor.

Photo courtesy: Getty Images.

Yoo-Hoo not only rolled off the tongue, but it was a marriage joined in endorsement heaven. He put the drink on the map and owned substantial stock in the company, at a time long before athletes struck major endorsement deals and earned big money as pitchmen.

He was treated like royalty when he visited the factory in Carlstadt, New Jersey. One time he was answering the phone at the factory, when a woman writing ad copy called to ask, "Is Yoo-Hoo hyphenated?" Yogi answered, "No, ma'am—it's not even carbonated!" That might have been the first in a long series of Yogi-isms that would bring him additional fame as a master of the malaprop.

After several changes in ownership, Yogi's connection to the drink had ended by the mid-1970s. Even the taste of the drink was different; in one year they changed the formula 26 times. But I always thought that Berra and Yoo-Hoo should be put back together. So when I was doing a project with Yoo-Hoo and I said, "We've gotta bring Yogi back." The new owners said, "It'll never happen." They cited the old ownership and stories and were sure the door was shut tight.

But I went straight to Yogi and his wife, Carmen. Because you never know until you try. It took me about two months to talk them into coming back. We talked about the heritage, the nostalgia, how people always loved the combination of Yogi and Yoo-Hoo. You never know, you keep working at it. It wasn't about the money—the Berras just wanted to make sure that the promotion was done the right way and that the campaign would go well. But it took time to find out their concerns and address them.

Over the course of two months, we made it happen. It ended up being one of Steiner Sports best promotions. It was a grand slam! We got so much publicity that Yoo-Hoo sales actually increased. People want things now, now, now, but sometimes if you take the time, if you find out the facts, you can really make great things happen.

We've gotten so used to instant this and instant that, most of us have forgotten that most things have to be grown—planted, watered, nurtured, and given time to mature. Only then can you harvest. I really believe that if you've got a chance to do something good, you should be willing to give it time and energy—because you never know.

YOU NEVER KNOW WHO WILL INSPIRE YOU

I want to leave you with one of my favorite "you never know" stories. Dave Winfield once said, "You never know where your next inspiration is going to come from." And this story is about him. Dave was voted to the Baseball Hall of Fame in 2001, making it in the most prestigious way possible—on the Baseball Writers of America Association's first ballot. Since then, Dave and I have had many dealings together, and I have found him to be one of the most articulate athletes to come down the pike.

Winfield joined the California Angels in 1990, leaving behind a sour relationship with New York Yankees owner George M. Steinbrenner III. "I felt better since I left," Dave said after departing New York. "I don't have gray hair anymore."

But even back then there was a major worry about his health. He had missed all of 1989 with a back operation. If he could not return to baseball in 1990, at 38 years old, he would have ended his career with 2,421 hits, 357 homers, and 1,438 runs batted in. Those are fine career

Dave Winfield is one of the first baseball players to form a charity for inner city kids: Say "No" to Drugs.

Photo courtesy: Getty Images.

totals but not great enough to be Hall of Fame markers. But he earned my respect and the respect of many baseball enthusiasts by putting up four great comeback seasons.

Over the next four years—with California, Toronto, and Minnesota—he hit 96 homers and knocked in 348 runs. He reached his 3,000th hit in 1993, and he finished his career with 3,110. He got his 400th homer in 1991 and finished with 465. He also got the game-winning hit for Toronto in the 1992 World Series against the Atlanta Braves. By the time he retired, he had the numbers to make him an "automatic" selection for the Hall.

When most people were ready to cast a 38-year-old athlete on the ash heap, Winfield snapped back with a torrid finish. More than 15,000 players have played Major League Baseball, and not even 200—less than 2 percent—are in the Hall of Fame. Now Dave is one of them. "You never know" is one of life's great truths.

——— *Chapter Review* ———

▶ Give everyone the red carpet treatment.

▶ Trust your instincts. Sometimes you have to go with your hunches.

▶ "No" doesn't always mean "no." Sometimes it means "I need more information."

Mark Messier, number 11 of the New York Rangers, is better known as "The Captain." He never shows a lack of leadership and focus.

𝒫reparation prevents piss-poor performance.

—Nolan Richardson, former University of Arkansas basketball coach,
during a television interview with Charlie Rose, 1994.

GET FOCUSED!

L et's deal with some practical matters. How does one become a champion? What are the day-to-day things that a person needs to learn and do in order to succeed? Now that you've made your way through the early chapters and adjusted your attitude to propel yourself to success, consider the next steps.

PREPARATION AND PROFESSIONALISM

When champion athletes go into training, they deprive themselves of certain pleasures in order to be the best at what they do. We're not talking about major sacrifices here—I'm not saying that you must become celibate or go on a special diet. I keep it simple, remember?

For example, when I was a boy, on school nights we did our homework, talked on the phone, watched TV, and went to bed early. That's the kind of simple regimen I'm talking about: being rested and prepared for the next day. If your friends are going out dancing on Wednesday night, you don't have to go with them. It's your choice as to whether you want to be one of the party crowd or one of the champions. Pay now, party later. The price is low and the party is better when you're a success, believe me.

Dress appropriately. Athletes have it easy when they go to work. It's pretty obvious what they're supposed to be wearing. St. Louis quarterback Kurt Warner would look pretty ridiculous trying to do his job in a navy blue business suit, and I'd look pretty foolish coming to my office in cleats and a Rams uniform. Every team has a uniform; some are just more apparent than others. In the business world, you need to learn what is appropriate for your workplace and your job.

One good rule: Dress for the job you want, not the one you have. You give people subconscious clues about who you are by how you dress. Color studies show brown is a friendly color, while navy blue and charcoal gray are considered power colors. The best way to apply this is to see how the people on the next level in your workplace dress, and go with that style. Upper management tends to dress in "power" colors.

I'm not what you'd consider a clothes horse. I dress casually more often than not, but if I've got an important meeting, I suit up. There's a clothing store in New York City that has a great advertising line: "Casual Fridays are for people with nothing better to do on Friday night." Observe successful people, and emulate the way they dress.

I'm not necessarily advocating a return of the three-piece suit, especially in the dead of August. But I sincerely hope that casual Fridays and casual dress haven't led people to be casual in their attitudes toward work.

The most important element of professionalism is maintaining a positive attitude. My mother taught my brothers and me about the importance of staying positive in business by telling us the following story:

"A farmer had two milk cows. One cow only gave half a bucket of milk a day, while the other gave a full bucket. Which one was worth more?"

We were no fools. "The one that gave a full bucket!" we exclaimed.

"But the one who gave a full bucket always kicked it over," Mom said, "and spilled every drop. Now, which cow was more valuable?"

So how's your attitude? Are you doing the job, then "kicking over the bucket" by being negative about it?

A professional not only speaks positively about his business, he or she also looks for the positive aspects in even the most negative circumstances. When events aren't going the way I want them to, I ask myself, "What's the lesson? What am I supposed to learn from this? How can I turn these situations around and make something good out of them?"

Being professional is a combination of how you act, how you look, how you speak, and how you think.

FOCUS AND PRACTICE

Tiger Woods started practicing his golf swing before he was five. Michael Jordan played basketball on the playgrounds of Wilmington, North Carolina, then honed his talents in high school (where, by the way, he was cut from the team as a sophomore) and college (where he played in an NCAA championship as a freshman) before becoming a pro. Wayne Gretzky's father, Walter, built him an ice rink in back of his home. When his friends would ask Wayne to join them at the movies or other group activities, he would decline. He skated from morning until night.

Professional athletes of every sport practiced and learned their craft long before they ever reached stardom. If you're going to be a champion, then you're going to have to be focused. I'm not talking about the money; I'm talking about the attitude and the knowledge that combine to form professionalism.

Don Smith, who runs the sports marketing program at New York University, was telling me about two encounters with Jack Kemp, the football player turned congressman. Smith was a reporter and one day saw Kemp, then a quarterback for the Buffalo Bills, at practice. Kemp was holding a football by the smooth side, not by the threads as you normally would. "Jack! Why are you holding the ball that way?" Smith asked. Kemp replied, "Well, in the heat of a game, you can't always get it by the threads. I like to practice this way too so I can be ready for any situation."

So Don wrote a story about how Jack practiced holding the ball on the smooth side so he could be prepared. Kemp's story is another example of true professionalism: Don't work only on the obvious stuff; look for the things that can blind-side you, and work on those, too!

Fifteen years later, Don ran into Jack Kemp, who at that time was a successful congressman, at a fund-raising dinner. "Mr. Kemp," Don said, "you probably don't remember me . . . ."

But Kemp interrupted him. "Don Smith!" Kemp exclaimed. "You did that article on how I used to hold the football!" The second Kemp anecdote explains a lot of his political success, how he was able to head the AFL Players Association from 1965 to 1970, to succeed as a member of Congress for 17 years, head the Department of Housing and Urban Development, and run for vice president in 1996. He remembers names, he remembers events, he *recognizes* others, and makes them feel important.

PRODUCT KNOWLEDGE

The more you know about your business, the better able you are to serve—and remember: You are in a service business. You need to know not only the nuts and bolts of what you do, but also as much as possible about what everyone else does. The more you know, the more you can do.

GETTING IN THE KNOW

NBA Hall of Famer Walt Frazier is a guy who knows the importance of gaining knowledge and making changes based on new knowledge. Most people aren't aware of this, because he broadcasts television games on the New York Knicks, Madison Square Garden cable channel by saying players are "drivin' and thrivin'" and employing other colorful rhymes like "There goes Iverson, weavin' and deceivin'" or "Tracy McGrady—thrillin' and drillin'." Broadcasters develop signature styles for how they make home run calls or announce a touchdown and Frazier was no different: Rhyming was Frazier's signature, a kind of mixture of sports and hip hop. But Frazier spends much time researching and looking into all the little things about his product—which happens to be 29 NBA teams and 348 players. He's a fine broadcaster not only because of the research and the knowledge that he brings to the table, but also because he brings his actual lived experience as a player. Frazier has become an accomplished public speaker, too.

A lot of players who go into broadcasting become part of what the late Red Barber critically called the "jockocracy in the booth," relying on their playing experience to get them through broadcasts. The Brooklyn Dodgers' announcer with the pleasing southern lilt in his voice, Barber didn't think his job was to be a "homer" and root for his team, but to describe the action as a neutral reporter. He made some of the most famous calls in baseball history—such as Al Gionfriddo's "back-back-back-back" grab against Joe DiMaggio in the 1947 World Series—and is still regarded as one of the greatest ever to call a game. According to Red, former players in the booth thought they already knew the game and didn't need to do much work to prepare. They didn't want to go the extra mile. Few people would have thought of Walt Frazier as a potential broadcaster, but he started with incredible insight and took the time to learn how to package it for an audience.

Broadcasters are more accepted by fans, if they have previously been popular players. Frazier had always been a tremendously colorful performer in New York and was nicknamed "Clyde" by Knicks trainer Danny Whelan because of the wide-brimmed hats that looked like the ones worn by Clyde Barrow in the hugely successful movie, *Bonnie and Clyde*. Frazier was one of the first players in the 1970s with an enormous salary. He lived in a swank bachelor pad with a mirror over his round bed and was a snazzy dresser who always appeared in full-length furs and au courant fashions, whether he was just walking the streets or in a restaurant or at a boxing match.

In another respect, broadcasting did not come easily to Frazier. He had struggled in school, becoming academically ineligible at Southern Illinois University, and was not considered very articulate in his playing days, when he was more known for his excellent play and colorful lifestyle off the court. But Frazier had a great desire to learn and, by reading *The New York Times* and other highbrow publications, consistently increased his vocabulary. He also committed himself to learning more and more about the game of basketball and about how people want to hear about the game.

Frazier and I first started working together back in 1984, seven years after he last played with the Knicks. He had been traded to the Cleveland Cavaliers, where he finished his career, but "Clyde" probably should have played his last game in New York, where he was a basketball god. I was the general manager of the Sporting Club on Hudson Street in New York, the first establishment that began a trend of sports bars and restaurants. I hired him because we needed a celebrity to draw customers and press to our downtown club. It was magic having him around; I really enjoyed marketing him. He was my idol as a kid. He had his mind made up that he was somehow going to get into broadcasting. I insisted he contact the New York Knicks management and he did. He began to re-create a relationship with the team where he'd been so successful before he was traded to Cleveland. By the late 1980s he was alternating doing games on radio and for the Knicks' Madison Square Garden channel.

Today, Walt Frazier enjoys a full life doing television for the New York Knicks in the largest media market in the world. Putting in the time to learn did it for him. Few people realize how much of a student he was and still is. The fundamental thing to remember is to grab every opportunity you have, to learn more about what you do, and what you want to do. Acquire all the knowledge you can, and learn where to get the rest.

Photo courtesy: Steiner Sports.
Walt "Clyde" Frazier announcing at Madison Square Garden.

An administrative assistant increases his or her value by learning as much as possible about the business, not just the tools and skills of the job description. A salesperson should know how, where, and with what the product being sold is manufactured. A waiter needs to visit the kitchen and learn about food preparation. Whatever you do, you need to know as much as possible about what you're doing. Read whatever you can, see whatever you can, and ask questions of your management. If you're the business owner, ask your suppliers about their products. You'll be gaining invaluable knowledge, and perhaps even helping the people you ask to learn a few things, too!

SELF-KNOWLEDGE

You should work on knowing your business inside and out, but if you don't know *you*, then you're going to have a hard time. The Greek philosopher Socrates said "know thyself" and thought that self-knowledge was the most important practical knowledge for a good life. It's also important knowledge for a good business life.

Contrary to what you read in a lot of self-help books, most people have inflated images of themselves. We complete a task, meet a deadline, or close a deal, and we think we walk on water, like we're the greatest thing since sliced bread. Most of us assume that we *are* good enough, and that we don't need to take a long, hard look in the mirror, but the truth is, however good we may be, each of us can stand some improvement.

The best sports stars are always looking for ways they can improve themselves. New York Giants' linebacker Harry Carson remembered that he had to make quantum leaps of improvement at every level—from Wilson High School in Florence, South Carolina, to South Carolina State University, to the New York Giants. Climbing this staircase of success, Carson found it became extraordinarily harder at each level, beginning with making the high-school team.

I'd been playing sandlot ball with my friends, and I thought, having gone through a growth spurt and having played sandlot ball, I had what it took to make the team. And when I went out for the team, it really was a shock to my system with the running, the exercise.

But Carson pushed himself at every level. Bill Arnsparger once pointed at Harry Carson, who was going through a set of tortuous agility drills all by himself. "There is a future star," the Giants' head coach said. Arnsparger was absolutely correct.

In the tradition of great defensive players—long a hallmark of New York Giants football—Carson, a fourth-round draft pick in 1976, was an outstanding player for the team for 13 seasons. Often, he was the only great player on a team that struggled through the first half of his NFL career.

Carson told me that with extra work over the years, he learned how to read what offenses were doing. He was a smallish 6-foot-2-inches, 240-pounder who played defensive lineman in college and had to learn a new position in the pros. Carson became an inside linebacker and a ferocious run stopper.

Harry Carson, the Giants' outstanding linebacker, played in nine Pro Bowls and helped New York win Super Bowl XXI.

Photo courtesy: Getty Images.

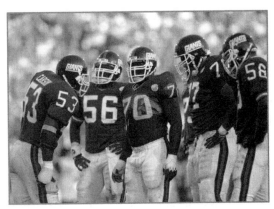

Known as the "Big Blue Wrecking Crew," the 1986 New York Giants led by Harry Carson (53) was one of the great defenses of all times.

Photo courtesy: Getty Images.

Later in his career, when he was joined by outside linebackers Lawrence Taylor and Carl Banks. There was no better line-backing trio in the NFL.

Like Taylor, Carson was difficult to stop man-for-man on blitzing pass rushes, and he had the speed and quickness to track down plays away from his position. He moved like a jungle cat after a runner or quarter-back. The Giants won Super Bowl XXI while Carson was playing and he appeared in nine Pro Bowls in his 13 NFL seasons. When he was fin-ished, he knew what had propelled him to success:

> I had to improve upon just about everything about my game. I mean in terms of your physical conditioning, every-thing. But for me, it was solely about commitment. And I think some people go into situations not fully committed, or they don't know what kind of commitment it takes to be suc-cessful.

FACING YOUR WEAKNESSES

I recall the day I discovered that I had to make the commitment because I didn't have the "goods" to succeed in business. I wanted to be a suc-cessful businessman, of course, but I didn't start out with wads of cap-ital, and I didn't have a family who could connect me with lots of movers and shakers. So I knew if I were to succeed, it would be because I had extraordinary commitment and drive.

Actually it wasn't a one-day revelation; there was a process involved. I had to understand more about the way I was and improve how I acted toward authority and not be so angry at taking orders from various bosses. I started my own self-help program, which included reading help books and going through a lot of self-evaluation. I would ask family and friends for painful feedback on the way I acted. Probably one of my biggest strengths is that I've come to realize the way I am: some of the things that I probably won't change, some of the things I can change, and some of the things I know I have changed. That's the biggest transition in beginning to become successful: starting to prey on *your own* weaknesses instead of the weaknesses of others; battling those things in yourself that you're not happy about.

There are a number of ways to discover your weaknesses. Some people sit down with a therapist for a couple of years. There's certainly nothing wrong with that; it may work. But if you've got a circle of close friends and family members, you can, subtly, over time, get some tremendous feedback.

Now, I don't think you should believe everything that everyone tells you. But I think when you hear the same message from different people who are not linked together, you should pay attention. In other words, if you ask three family members who live with you the same question, you'll probably get some similar answers. That may not be the whole picture, though, because those people are talking to each other. When a family member, a friend, and someone at work all say the same thing about you, then that's a pretty good clue to your true self.

My grandmother had an old Yiddish saying: "If one person tells you that you're drunk, ignore him. If two people tell you you're drunk, stop drinking. But if three people tell you that you're drunk, for God's sake, lie down."

When you learn about group dynamics, you hear about sitting down and opening yourself up and being available to hear everything, including the good, the bad, and the ugly. Sometimes you can be open to a coworker, or someone you work for, and you can ask, "What do you think my biggest weakness is?" I think you can ask that with anyone who knows you well, as long as there's no hidden agenda.

Your attitude and timing are very important if you really want to get accurate feedback. When someone tells you about your "dark side," there can't be repercussions. If somebody's going to tell you how he or she feels, then you can't suddenly get angry and snap back. That can change the dimensions of your relationship—and not for the better. First of all, you want the information, but you also want to leave the door open for a second stage where you can go back to those people to ask if they think you're changing. You're going to need to go back to those people, and if you get huffy with them when they told you what they think, they certainly aren't going to be eager to help you later on.

I had many people willing to give me guidance, and not all of it was immediately welcome. My mom helped me a lot with this, and I had some pretty serious, intense bosses who really didn't care how I felt. They gave me some painful feedback. I guess you have a tendency to dislike bosses like that, but when you look back, those are the people you remember because they told it to you the way it was. I tend to be that kind of boss. Some employees have had a certain dislike for me as a boss; when I've asked why, they say it's because I was too tough, or mean, but when you break that down, it's because I told them the truth—because I told them what nobody else wanted to tell them. Look back and see which bosses taught you the most about yourself.

Another way to learn about yourself is to go back into some of your failures. Look at some of the places where you haven't been successful and try to figure out why. Review those situations by yourself, and, when possible, with the people who were there at the time. Do an

PUSHING PEOPLE'S BUTTONS

I know the way I am. I've always been a person to stir up the dust. I'm always going to be the master of what it takes to get under somebody's skin. I walk around my office, and I know exactly what it takes to push people's buttons, and sometimes I don't care about the aftermath. I walk away afterward and they're all huffy and puffy, and meanwhile the energy level hits the ceiling.

Bubba told me that every football team has "a guy on the line who has a little thug in him." Bubba Smith was an enormous—6-feet-7-inches, 265 pounds—and dominant defensive end and tackle with the Baltimore Colts as a rookie in 1967. He played on two Baltimore teams that made it to the Super Bowl and had a ten-year career in a league where the average is only four years. Bubba describes the thuggish guy like this: "That thug, you know, when the game gets close and you want to give up, you think they're overtaking you, he's the one who says, "Hey, what the f— is going on here? Are we just gonna give it up? Are you crazy?"

Bubba gives the perfect example of this "thug" when he talks about playing at Michigan State with Charles "Mad Dog" Thornhill.

"We were playing Notre Dame, the famous 10–10 game," Bubba told me. "It came to a point where it was third and long, and the whole stadium, about 85,000 people, all of them started yelling, 'Kill, Bubba, Kill,' and Dog, the thug, he looked at me and he said, "They're cheering for you, why don't you do something?" So I said, "Hey man, f— you." I knew what he was doing, but sometimes you need to hear that, to lift you out of your funk."

I see myself as being a little like "Mad Dog" sometimes. I did something similar a while ago with one of my employees. I asked him the same question three times in an hour and a half, which I knew would totally annoy him, and then I came back 15 minutes later and asked him again. He finally came into my office and blew up, which was great and was exactly what I wanted. I wanted him to get that spirit, that energy level. I wanted to get him angry. And he went crazy all day, had a phenomenal day. So I'm one hell of an instigator when I need to be, but that's what it took to get him going.

Most people think they're way ahead of where they really are and don't want to examine their weaknesses. I'm only interested in my weaknesses. I just want to know about the problems; I don't need anybody to tell me how great I am. That's not going to help me. It's nice to hear it once in a while, but generally I thrive on, "What do we need to do? What's lacking?" That interests me.

Knowing the way you are is difficult. Then the next step is deciding whether you want to stay that way or not

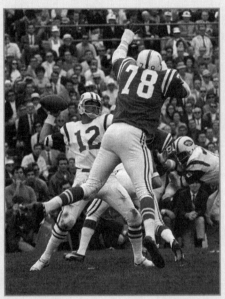

Photo courtesy: AP Worldwide.

Bubba Smith, number 78, leaps to try and block a pass from Jets quarterback Joe Namath in Super Bowl III in Miami. The Jets won that game 16 to 7.

You've probably already figured this out, but I have to point out here that confidence is not one of my weak spots. If your confidence level needs work, then build it before any self-analysis. One way to build self-confidence is to instill confidence in others. Once you're ready to take a look at yourself, evaluate which parts of your demeanor and your attitude are wrong and which are right. Sometimes it takes great self-awareness just to know what you're doing *right*.

honest self-appraisal. See what the causes were. Fear? Self-doubt? Did you not want to rock the boat? Or was it something else? Learn the way you are by examining your mistakes and seeing what you left out.

BUILDING ON YOUR STRENGTHS

Knowing yourself includes knowing the best time of day for yourself. If you're not a morning person, don't place your most important responsibilities in the early part of the day. I very rarely schedule early morning meetings. I *am* a morning person, but I don't like people in my face before noon. I like to take care of my task-oriented responsibilities in the morning and do creative stuff in the afternoon.

Know how you are. If you're not good with money, let your partner handle it.

Know what food makes you buzz and what brings you down. It doesn't matter how much you like a certain food, if it makes you soporific, don't eat it before a business meeting. As Gordie Howe said, a key for him was finding out the foods that worked for him personally, not just what doctors or nutritionists said.

Know what your heart rate should be so you can efficiently do aerobic exercises. And don't overexercise. Those of us who get to a "certain age" can't push it too far—that's abusive.

The better you know yourself, the better you'll be able to advance in every area of your life. Knowing yourself helps you know what you want and what you need. That will make it easier for you to live with yourself and ultimately for others to live with you.

Know who you are, what you want, what obstacles you put in your own path and work on removing them. And remember that removing those obstacles is not just bending over and picking up a piece of paper. Sometimes you have to get a bulldozer.

It's difficult to take a bad trait and work for change, especially with someone like me, who tried to be a tough kid. Roaming the streets of Brooklyn, my guard was always up. Walking down the street I was often thinking, "Who am I going to get into a fight with?" "Who's looking to take what I have?" "How can I get what I need to survive?" I was one big, walking defense mechanism.

As a kid, even through college, my theme was "survive." Just to get through whatever I was going through. It was a long time before I could change "survive" into "thrive." I kept hearing, "Brandon, you're just too tough, loosen up!" I'm probably still too tough, but I'm much more tender than I used to be. It hasn't been easy.

Some people are the opposite, and too soft is just as bad. Either way, you have to know who you are and keep aware of it in situations with other people. No relationship really ends happily; if it was happy, it wouldn't end. Examine difficulties with others and see what your part is. That's the part over which you have some control.

When you need help in dealing with others, there are a number of books that help you to know who you are and give you some support in learning how to deal with people. This is one of those, and others are listed under Suggested Reading at the end of this book.

—— *Chapter Review* ——

▸ Find your niche and pursue it with passion.

▸ Be prepared for whatever the next day will bring. Be rested and be dressed appropriately.

▸ Maintain a professional, positive attitude.

▸ Learn everything you can about your business and the businesses you deal with.

▸ You may know a lot, but do you know yourself?

After 54 years of trying, the New York Rangers finally stopped their slide. Mike Keenan's focus and drive led the Rangers to win the 1994 Stanley Cup.

f you want to make enemies, try to change something.

—Woodrow Wilson, 28th President of the United States.

NOTHING CHANGES
IF NOTHING CHANGES

This principle can be summed up in one sentence: If you always do what you've always done, then you'll always get what you've always had. *Dynamic dissatisfaction* is what drives the process of regularly making changes even when everything seems to be "good enough." We'll talk more about dynamic dissatisfaction later in this chapter.

Most people have a mindset that says, "If it ain't broke, don't fix it." That's not how I look at the world. I say, "If it ain't broke, break it." That's my style. I never want things to stay the same; I'd get stale that way. I believe if you want to make things better, you've got to get underneath them, crack them open, and get inside.

Waiting for things to get better by themselves is like watching the grass grow. Champions have better things to do. My friend A.J. Richards started PC Richards, a discount appliance store, that is now a wildly successful chain of appliance stores. A.J. said to me, "Sometimes you have to make a bigger mess in order to clean things up."

This chapter is about gaining new perspectives and staying fresh. "If it ain't broke, break it" because routines and comfort levels create laziness. You see it every day: People find too much comfort in their routines, and they tend to want to do less. I believe that's human nature, whether people are aware of it or not.

You've got to stay out of the routine because routines don't help you grow. Shuffle the cards! Every time you shuffle the cards, you get a new hand, and you get to deal with that hand differently. Sometimes it brings you to the same result, but you become more experienced, smarter about how to handle different things instead of being a machine operator or an order-taker. If you want to be on top of your game, you've got to keep handing in your cards and getting a new set. It would be nice to hold onto a good little hand and never let go, but we all know that's not how the game is played.

If you're getting the same results year in and year out, you have to realize that to get a different result, you have to change what you're doing—even if you're doing it right! Because nothing changes if nothing changes. If you mix milk and chocolate syrup, you'll always get chocolate milk. If you want a milk shake, you're going to have to add ice cream. You're going to have to change the formula.

GET A NEW PERSPECTIVE

Now take an example from history. In the Old West, some Native American tribes believed people should sit close to the fire, not just for warmth, but for what visions could be seen in the fire. But cowboys believed in sitting away from the fire, in order to be more alert to sights and sounds around them while staying reasonably warm. It's not a question of the right way or the wrong way; it's a matter of perspective.

MASTER OF CHANGE

B ehold his Airness, Michael Jordan. People will parrot the idea that Michael Jordan is the greatest basketball player that ever lived. But how many of them have examined why that is? Statistics alone tell part of the story. He has won ten scoring titles, has the highest points-per-game average of all time (30.3) and the highest average in playoffs (33.4). Defense? He was selected for the NBA All-Defensive First Team nine times. And of course, he played on six championship teams with the Chicago Bulls.

But how did he do all this? Did he achieve so much by standing pat? No. When he came into the NBA he could drive and leap with the best ever, hence his nickname "Air Jordan." But he didn't have a consistent perimeter game, so he worked on perfecting his outside shot. He also had to learn to trust his teammates more and bring them into the game. He did, working Scottie Pippen, John Paxson, and others into the picture, bringing Chicago NBA titles in 1991, 1992, and 1993.

He was a dogged competitor long before he came to the NBA. Discipline was a constant in Jordan's life. His career is over, but the lessons of his career—and how he faced challenges—will always be there for people to observe. Jordan worked and worked, overcoming the setback of being cut as a sophomore from the Laney High varsity team in Wilmington, North Carolina. Then assistant coach Fred Lynch explained, "We thought he'd be better off playing on the JV team. He didn't sulk, he worked."

"He never wanted to lose in anything," said his physical education teacher, Ruby Sutton. "That was born into him. I normally got to school between 7:00 and 7:30 in the morning; Michael would get there at 6 A.M. I'd hear the ball bouncing—fall, winter, summer. I had to chase him from the gym."

Jordan made varsity his junior year. Two years later, he was playing basketball for the University of North Carolina. In his freshman year, he hit a game-winning shot with just seconds remaining to beat Georgetown and give Carolina the NCAA title. "Hitting that shot as a snot-nosed kid, I always had the confidence later on," Jordan said. He was really saying that the success he achieved would help him to succeed later.

But those successes didn't come without adversity. The challenges kept presenting themselves, even as he worked to improve himself. Not only did he improve his jump shot, but even while scoring a load of points, his shooting percentage stayed above 50 percent—which is a rarity for guards in the NBA. But before long, he had been in the league for six years and still hadn't won a championship. Now he heard the talk. It was the usual stuff about how individual players can't play on a winner. He heard the criticisms that he was just a "solo act" and couldn't mesh with a cast of characters who would also be subordinate to him and not able to flourish

The Detroit Pistons, NBA champions for consecutive years, made no secret that they would play the Bulls by employing the "Jordan Rules," which basically meant they would collapse on him and bang him around whenever he touched the ball. They exacted a toll on his body, steering him into traffic and roughing him up whenever possible. The excessively physical brand of basketball often left Jordan on the floor. That left the other Bulls to step up and win games, but for years they couldn't rise to the task.

But winning a title became Jordan's major goal. First, his coach Phil Jackson told him, he would have to learn to trust his teammates and not think of himself as the only player who could succeed under pressure. Jackson applied to basketball what he called a "Zen Christian" attitude of selfless awareness. Jackson opted for assistant Tex Winter's "triangle offense," a spread-out attack that would utilize more players' skills with proper spacing and crisp passing. The Bulls now got crucial help from Scottie Pippen, Horace Grant, John Paxson, and B.J. Armstrong.

With this more rounded effort, Chicago beat Detroit to win the Eastern Conference in 1991 and then went on to beat the Los Angeles Lakers for the Bulls' first NBA title. But many teams win single NBA titles. So it was important to Jordan that the team win again. They did, and then they won again the next year, making it three in a row. He should have been on top of the world, but just two months after the third consecutive title, his father was murdered.

Jordan shook up a lot of things after his father died, retiring in 1993. But he returned 18 months later—after playing baseball in the Chicago White Sox farm system—although he had to shake off the rust to get into "basketball shape." After he had retired he was considered the greatest player in the game, perhaps ever. But it took being away from the game he loved to discover how much he missed it. He wasn't returning to the game to be an also-ran.

Then at 32, he thought he needed to spend more time with weights to build his strength. He worked furiously over the summer, and the Bulls won a world title, and set a record with 72 wins in 1996. Then they won 69 games the next year and brought Chicago two more titles.

Anyone watching Jordan closely knew just how much he changed his game. Over the years, he developed a "fadeaway" jumper to compensate for some of his reduced flight time. He wasn't exactly "Ground Jordan," but he wasn't accumulating as many frequent flier miles either. He also knew when to catch a rest during games so he would still have his energy for the end. To play long and to play well, even Michael Jordan had to rethink the way he did things.

Jordan retired from the Washington Wizards in 2003 after a second comeback two years before. Even in returning he was willing to take risks. Some argued that he would degrade his reputation as the greatest player of all time. But he still loved the sport, didn't need the money—he donated his salary to a charity for victims of the World Trade Center attacks—could deliver the occasional big game, and teach his younger mates about how to approach the game. After Washington lost a game against New York in which Jordan scored 39 points, he chastised his mates for not making the same effort that he, at 40 years old, had made. Weeks earlier he became the first player older than 40 to score 40 points in a game. He was no longer the NBA's king of the hill, but he was still a force with seconds remaining and the game hanging in the balance.

His willingness to make changes made him in many ways more intriguing than ever, despite the fact that his best years were behind him. Once the king of the court, he remained the king of endorsements, with the highest Q-Rating among any athlete. A maestro could not have made the changing parts of his career fit together any better.

Chicago Bulls' Michael Jordan holds the NBA Championship trophy after the Bulls beat the Seattle SuperSonics 87 to 75 on June 16, 1996, in Chicago. It was Chicago's fourth NBA Championship.

Photo courtesy of Associated Press Worldwide.

I think there are any number of changes you can make just to get a new perspective. Even little changes that seem mundane can make a big difference. If you've been sitting in the same office and at the same desk for a few years, try switching offices with somebody or at least re-arranging your furniture. I move my people at Steiner Sports about once or twice a year. It costs money, but my people learn new things and stay fresh. Give yourself and your people something new from time to time. It takes a person about six months to get settled into a new pattern, and then in 18 months, they're stale.

One of Jordan's former teammates on several of those championship teams, B.J. Armstrong, recalls how coach Phil Jackson would give all the Bulls books to read to keep their minds active. And when they came to stay at the Plaza Hotel in New York, Jackson would ask the bus driver to take varied routes from Central Park South to Madison Square Garden, where they would play the Knicks, just to give his players a different perspective.

MAKE LITTLE CHANGES

Changes, though, need to be evolutionary, not revolutionary. You might be reading this book on a Sunday night and have a sudden burst of enthusiasm and inspiration. "I'm gonna change the way I do *everything* tomorrow!" you say, or you might think, "I'm going to improve all my processes and work smarter, faster," and so on. Let's say that you do. Your employer is likely to have one of two reactions: "Why weren't you working like this before?" or "How long will this last?" Neither one is a good response.

Most of us know we need improvement, but we think we have to "fix" ourselves all at once, instead of making small changes.

Rather than trying to change everything all at once, make change a part of your game plan. Make changes one at a time and plan the next few as you go. Change your behavior the way a company changes its pricing structure—incrementally. A manufacturing company would never tell its customers, "We've been undercharging you for years, so now we're going to raise the price 100 percent!" That's a good way to chase off a customer. Instead, the business makes a series of small increases in price.

Make sure your incremental changes in behavior can be maintained. Most diets fail because they're quick fixes, not changes in behavior or lifestyle. I could lose a lot of weight eating nothing but plain baked potatoes. But how long could I possibly keep that up? You can impress your customers, your boss, and everyone else by working 16- to 18-hour days, but you're likely to crash and burn if you're not used to that pace.

I tell my employees all the time, "I know you're working hard, but if you want a different result, you're going to have to do something differently. What are you going to do differently?" If you want to make changes, maybe you need to go into the office one Saturday a month to reshuffle, take a look, and make sure you're using your time correctly. Look into the file system of your computer. Do you have a bunch of old, useless files cluttering your hard drive and slowing your system? Delete them. Are stacks of papers and files covering the desk and chairs in your office? File them or get rid of them. You'll feel less overwhelmed and more in control.

OFTEN, IT'S THE LITTLE THINGS

Maybe you need to dress differently. If you're a business owner, maybe it's time to change your logo. We do it every so often. Sometimes just changing the font you use for your letters makes a difference. It's all about shaking things up.

Try switching the type of pen you use. Michael Jordan said he used a new pair of sneakers every game. He said there's nothing like the feeling you get from a new pair of sneakers. Of course, this was also one of

Jordan's ways to stay prepared, because he began this practice after he broke his foot during his second year in the NBA and had to miss 64 games. Besides getting a great feeling from a new pair of sneakers, he also knew that his shoes were at their sturdiest.

Nothing like the first week in a new office, nothing like finding a new pen that you enjoy writing with. Sometimes these things are like a brand new day. I can't stress it enough—making changes gets you out of ruts. People have asked me how I come up with so many ideas all the time; I think it's a direct result of continually making little changes. It keeps the brain active.

STRIVE FOR DYNAMIC DISSATISFACTION

In terms of management, when Steiner Sports is doing its best and sales are up, is when most people relax, and that's when I feel like I really have to jump in. I think most people are sensitive enough to know that when things are down, they have to work harder, but it's when things are really good, that I feel I have to manage the most. That's when many people get cocky, start looking for shortcuts, and spend unnecessarily.

It's harder to find the mistakes when things are good. I just bought a sports collectibles store called Hall of Heroes from a friend of mine. It's in the Roosevelt Field Mall in Long Island,

No matter how well Paul O'Neil of the New York Yankees did, he always expected to do better.

Photo courtesy: Getty Images.

New York. It is the number two mall in the country; an excellent location for a store. My friends told me that the good location lets many mistakes stay hidden. If the store's location were poorer, I'd probably keep my eyes open wider to problems such as overstaffing and overstocking. But because of the store's volume, many potential problems could be easily overlooked. The usual attitude is, "We're making so much money, what the hell." Those are the times when I want to squeeze! Some of our biggest deals have come when instead of saying, "Wow, look how much we're making," I said, "We're making at least this much money; can we make more?" I don't put a ceiling on myself.

It's not about greed; I'm not trying to squeeze the customer. I'm trying to squeeze my company. How much more can we do? What other services can we offer? I've learned that it's a lot easier and a lot more profitable to serve an existing customer than to find a new customer.

Some of my employees say, with a slight edge in their voices, "It's never good enough for Brandon!" It's true. I'm never satisfied. But just because I'm not satisfied, it doesn't mean I'm not happy! There's a big difference between what I call dynamic dissatisfaction and frustrated unhappiness.

I always look at it like I haven't accomplished anything yet. I saw actor Robin Williams in a TV interview recently. A reporter asked, "When you look back at your career, what is your defining moment?" Williams said, "I haven't found it yet." Even after numerous hit movies and career accolades, Williams is still expecting better things for himself. I look at this and think, "We've built this whole business; what's your defining moment, and how are you going to be remembered?" And I think that I'm not happy with it yet; I'm not there yet.

Dynamic dissatisfaction is about constantly upgrading your goals. Mike Keenan, who has played in Stanley Cup championships and coached a couple of championship hockey teams, says, "True champions set high standards for themselves and the people around them, and constantly readjust their goals and expectations."

I think one of the saddest things in the world is when someone reaches a major goal and stops. Go as far as you can see, and you'll always be able to see farther. As soon as you can see farther, resolve to go there! Sure, it's OK to rest on your laurels for a little while, but if you're not careful, you can get buried under them.

Ask yourself regularly what you can do differently, what small changes you can make, how you might shake things up just a little. Keep in mind that making mistakes is part of the process. You'll never be bored, and you just might come up with something brilliant!

There's an old saying: Behold the turtle—he only makes progress when he sticks his neck out.

—— *Chapter Review* ——

▶ Make changes in your routine to get a fresh perspective.

▶ Search for new perspectives.

▶ Make change incremental, long-lasting.

▶ Look at the little things.

▶ Dynamic dissatisfaction can lead to success.

Billie Jean King celebrates one of her six Wimbledon crowns.

*A*dversity weakens the weak and strengthens the strong.

—Anonymous.

IT'S NOT WHAT HAPPENS TO YOU, IT'S WHAT YOU DO WITH WHAT HAPPENS

Those of us who have lived for a time know one truth all too well. If you travel the road of success, you're going to meet adversity at many spots along the way. You'll even come across failure a few times. The key is to keep going and look for new ways to reach your goals. As longtime Los Angeles Dodgers manager Tommy Lasorda says, "The difference between the possible and the impossible lies in a person's determination."

If you don't believe it, ask Billie Jean King. King ruled: she dominated women's professional tennis for a decade, beginning in the mid-1960s. She won the prestigious singles title 12 times, including six times at Wimbledon. She also won 27 doubles events, giving her 39 Grand Slam titles—the third highest total of all time.

Despite the success on the court, she is known more for being a trailblazer off the court. Early in her life she realized she would have to overcome the significant obstacles that all women athletes had to face in the 1950s and 1960s.

> When I was 12 (in 1955) I had an epiphany. I was sitting alone in the Los Angeles Tennis Club, on the grandstand court. The sun was setting and I was all by myself. From the time I was 11 I understood that, as a girl, I was discounted. I didn't yet understand it fully, but thoughts were bubbling. I already got the picture that I was a second-class citizen, but I didn't fully realize it until I was 17. I just knew things weren't right. I liked playing team sports, but tennis was very elitist. I wasn't allowed in a photo when I was 11 because I was wearing shorts, instead of a skirt or a dress. In my first sanctioned tournament the guys told me I couldn't be in a photo-op—just stupid things like that. I got to thinking how I loved track and field, softball, basketball, baseball, and thought that tennis needs to be like them—it needs to be more hospitable. I already knew it was a stuffy, elitist sport and I didn't like it. I could play tennis and I knew that it was international and that I could get an education by traveling and meeting fantastic people. It gave me a chance to run, jump, and hit. And I liked running in different directions, like basketball. And I got to hit a ball and God gave me great reflexes, so I found it the most fun. You get a great workout.

But her epiphany didn't make for clear sailing the rest of the way.

When she enrolled in Cal State Los Angeles, she had already won a Wimbledon title and was the most famous person on campus. But the college didn't give her an athletic scholarship. It would have been understandable if the college refused her a scholarship on the grounds that she was a professional. But she wasn't; women tennis players were still amateurs. No one college was to blame: Athletic scholarships simply weren't available for women.

King began to work toward making changes for women in sports in the early 1970s. King and Donna De Varona, a gold medal swimmer from the 1964 Olympics, went to testify before a Senate committee. Their efforts ensured that the Education Amendment, especially the Title IX portion of the bill, was passed by Congress. Title IX bans sex discrimination in schools, whether in academics or athletics.

Then came "The Battle of the Sexes." In 1973 Bobby Riggs challenged King to a match that would be covered on national television. King throttled Riggs in straight sets—6–4, 6–3, 6–3. "It was very symbolic of what we were tying to do," King said. "We were trying to get athletic scholarships for women."

Her efforts kept paying dividends. She fought a pitched battle to get women equal tournament pay. She went in to see tournament official and former player Bill Talbert. "We got the money even with what the men were paid in 1973 because we had Clairol as a sponsor waiting in the wings," King recalls. "When I went in to talk to Bill, I didn't go in scared. I just said to Bill, 'I think women draw as well as men do. We had a sponsor that would make up the difference in pay between men and women.' Talbert agreed and women's tournament purses would be comparable to men's for the first time.

With world-class play on the court and landmark contributions off, King, to no one's surprise, was one of few athletes to appear on lists at both *Sports Illustrated* and *Sport* as the 40 most important athletes of the century in the mid-1980s. She believes her lasting contribution in the game comes from "what I did off the court." As great a player as she was, how great she could have been is unknown to her.

> I never really had a chance to know what I could be as a player. We were in meetings all night long. We were trying to get sponsors just to get players to appear in a match. How many players have to do that? When we were starting the women's tour in 1971, we were up all night. I was doing interviews until

2 A.M., in meetings until 4 A.M., because we had to keep pushing forward. Then we went out and played the following afternoon. As a player, it was more of a sanctuary for me to go play
a match. It didn't bother me for a minute.

King likes to say, "It is each generation's job to push the next." She
means that "Women's sports are still in their infancy" and there are
still miles to go. She notes how the quality of play in the Women's
2003 NCAA Basketball final between Tennessee and Connecticut was
far greater than five years ago. "As I was watching, I was thinking,
'This is nothing yet. They're going to be so much better in another
five to ten years.'"

Another of King's favorite sayings is, "The more you know about
history, the more you know about yourself."

It means, for instance, when I walked onto the center-
court at Wimbledon, or the U.S. Open, or on the WTA Tour if
I were younger, if I was starting now, I would know the history
of every player, or at least the top players. It puts perspective
into the game. I knew when the game started, knew how long
it had been around, how long the women and men had been
doing what they were doing. I knew that the Davis Cup
Tournament started for men in 1900 but for women it was
1963—63 years behind the men in promotion and tradition,
things that add up over time. To know the history made it
more exciting and gave me empathy for the past and the people who paid the price before me. And it makes a difference in
your play at times if you have a positive thought and it uplifts
you at times during a match. You understand your match is
part of history and it helps you to see the meaning of it all and
what kind of legacy you want to leave in your life.

I think some players still have this historical awareness.
Someone in the press said to Venus Williams, "You're the first

African American woman to be ranked number one in the world." Venus corrected her: "No Althea Gibson was the first; they just didn't have computer rankings back then." Because Venus knew her history, she knew Althea was first, and that Arthur Ashe was the first man and second African American overall to be ranked number one. But the press at times isn't very old and they don't know the history themselves.

Women who don't know King's history surely don't know how they got where they are. Trailblazers such as Jackie Robinson, Gibson, King, and Arthur Ashe—always take their lumps. But look at what they did in their own careers and for others. King is still fighting for women's equality of opportunity through her association with Women's Team Tennis and the Women's Sport Foundation, which she helped begin in 1974. Obstacles were put in her path. But look at how she went past those obstacles. It's not what happens to you, it's what you do with what happens.

I believe that I've learned more from my failures than I have from my successes. I think we all do. When copywriters at Nike were searching for the right words for a commercial with Michael Jordan, he grew impatient with them and said, "Is someone paying you for this time?" People laughed. He then came up with the line himself. "I have failed many times, and that is why I succeed," Jordan said.

Smooth sailing doesn't teach us much, or as my good friend Yogi Berra said, "If the world was perfect, it wouldn't be."

I once asked Derek Jeter if he would have changed anything in his life; he hardly hesitated before saying, "Not at all. You have to fail before you can succeed, and I've failed a lot. People talk about my overnight success and all that stuff, but I've had a lot of failures in the minor leagues. People don't know that I committed 56 errors in my second year." The Yankees have won four World Series in the eight years he has played on the team, but that means there were four other years they didn't win. Jeter had to resolve to learn from those defeats.

OVERCOMING THE NAYSAYERS

The first roadblock most of us have to overcome is opposition from the people who say "no." Often these aren't our enemies—very often they're the people who care about us the most, the people who don't want to see us get hurt. Just remember, however, good their intentions, the "no" people are people who believe you can't do it. I don't mean that you should take their opposition personally—that would be a mistake, because "no" says more about the naysayer than it does about you.

I love football legend Jim Brown's attitude. Brown played fullback for nine years for the Cleveland Browns before leaving the game in 1965 and going off to Hollywood to make *The Dirty Dozen* and a load of other films. In his nine years, he won the NFL rushing title an unprecedented eight times. His 5.2 yards per carry is the all-time best and he is still regarded as the greatest runner who ever played. Jim is the kind of man who gets motivated when people tell him "no," and in his career the "no" people seemed to be all around him. "When I went into professional football," Jim says, "they told me I couldn't average over five yards per carry. They told me that 1,000 yards for 12 games was great,

Cleveland Browns fullback Jim Brown busts through the New York Giants line, sweeps wide for four yards and a record-breaking touchdown, October 4, 1965. It was Brown's 106th career touchdown, breaking the mark held by Green Bay's Don Hutson. Brown scored two more touchdowns in victory over New York.

Photo courtesy: Steiner Sports.

and I said, "No, 1,000 yards for 12 games is not great, it's not even 100 yards per game!"

Doing the things that seem impossible, overcoming adversity, and coming back from defeat usually takes tremendous effort. More often, it takes tremendous desire and, as NBA star-turned-coach Isiah Thomas says, the ability to "use negative experiences as a springboard."

When I asked Ernie Banks how he managed to overcome the negative comments of others, especially during his early days as one of the first two black players on the Chicago Cubs, this is what he said: "My father, Satchel Page, Buck O'Neill, Gene Baker, Jackie Robinson, all told me: 'Sticks and stones will break your bones, but words will never hurt.' So I kinda live by that, at the beginning of my life and now. I'm not a philosopher—but I would advise people to love many, trust few, and paddle your own canoe."

I hadn't heard those words about sticks and stones since I was a boy, but Ernie lives by them, day after day. He became famous for his sunny disposition. He'd look up at a sunny Chicago sky and say, "It's a great day for baseball, so let's play two." His success as a player, during the 1950s with a perennial last-place team, owes much to his persistence. Usually MVPs aren't given to those performing on last-place clubs. But Ernie won back-to-back MVPs—the only shortstop ever to do that—in 1958 and 1959. Before the present-day explosion in home-run hitting, endurance, and daily stick-to-itiveness was needed to hit 500 homers in a career. In a career that ended in 1971, Banks hit 512 homers.

OVERCOMING THE ODDS

Tommy Lasorda, manager of the Dodgers for 20 years, tells a great story about overcoming what seemed to be insurmountable odds. "In 1988 we had played against the Mets 11 times, and they beat us 10 times. Our 12th game was rained out, and I have to say I was very happy about that.

GO WITH WHAT WORKS

have come to know Mia Hamm through her association with Steiner Sports. As I've said earlier, Mia is one the world's best all-around women's soccer player. At 15 she became the youngest woman ever to play with the U.S. National Team. In 1989 she won her first of four NCAA titles with the University of North Carolina. She was just 19 when she appeared on the United States world championship team. When she completed her collegiate career in 1993 she was the all-time conference leader in goals scored, assists, and points. In 1999 she became the all-time scoring leader in international soccer with her 108th goal. She was also a member of the 1996 and 2000 U.S. Olympic teams.

Photo courtesy: Getty Images.

Being the best in a sport that is just now coming into its own, Mia has faced her share of adversity and offers this advice on coping with it: "When something negative happens, you need to analyze your response and see if it works. Is getting angry effective? Does pretending nothing happened work for you? You need to find out what within yourself pushes you ahead."

I asked Mia how she personally reacts to adversity, and

you might be surprised at her answer. "I get very angry," she said. She said her anger gets her extremely focused and helps her to "go after it" more intensely. Mia reminded me that not everyone works that way: for most people, anger is a drawback. I agree: I've seen anger, even heated rage, compound—not alleviate—problems for most people. But people tick differently. And each person has to find what helps him or her get through adversity without making matters worse.

But when we played them in the playoffs, I told the team we were going to beat them because we wanted it a little bit more than they did. We beat them in a very tough seven-game series."

Lasorda, like Red Auerbach, is a great motivator. When it was discovered that David Cone, one of the Mets' star pitchers, had written a guest column in the *New York Daily News* stating that the Dodgers didn't have much of a hitting attack, Lasorda used Cone's slight for motivational fodder. Again, when the team was about to play the Oakland Athletics in the 1988

Riding umpires was one of Tommy Lasorda's pasttimes. Here he argues during the 2000 Olympics, when he led the United States to a gold medal.

Photo courtesy: Getty Images.

World Series, a broadcaster claimed that the Dodgers' lineup was the weakest he'd seen in a long time, maybe the worst ever to compete in a World Series. Again, Lasorda used such comments as a motivational charge to his troops.

In Game 1 of the Series Oakland held a 4 to 3 lead with two men out in the night inning. The Dodgers' most consistent performer and National League MVP that year, Kirk Gibson, was dressed in street clothes as the game began. With a severely pulled left hamstring and strained ligaments in his right knee, Gibson could barely walk. But as the Dodgers fell behind in the game, Gibson donned his uniform and limped to a batting cage beneath the stands in Dodger Stadium.

With a man on first base, Lasorda summoned Gibson to pinch hit. Relief ace Dennis Eckersley blew two fastballs by him. On the next pitch—swinging on one leg—Gibson was able to get the bat around on a slower breaking pitch and hit it over the right field fence. The Dodgers had stolen a game and it changed the tide of the World Series. The Dodgers rolled to an easy five-game victory and a World Championship no one thought they could win. Gibson had made the most of adversity, preparing himself just in case a situation arose where he could contribute.

Most every successful business has been at a point where it was near failure, and mine is no exception. My close call came when we'd been in business for about four and a half years. Most of our business at the time came from selling closed-circuit fights to sports bars—setting up promotions where the bar would have the fight on the TV and a celebrity or two in the place watching the fight with you. We had put a lot of time, energy, and money into building this aspect of the business for about a year and a half, and a huge fight was coming up—the first Holyfield-Tyson bout. It was the fight of the decade; everyone wanted to see it. I had about $200,000 worth of business booked. High-level locations, corporations throwing their own private fight parties—I was into it hook, line, and sinker. I had put a lot of money into it myself—a lot of advertising, direct mail, things like that. Then the

FIRST NAME: _____ LAST NAME:_____ DATE OF BIRTH: ___ / ___ / _____

ADDRESS: _____

CITY: _____ STATE: _____ ZIP:_____

DAY PHONE: _____ EVENING PHONE: _____

☐ YES! PLEASE SEND ME SPECIAL OFFERS FROM *ENTREPRENEUR.*

EMAIL: (OPTIONAL) _____

ENTREPRENEUR PRESS "THERE'S NO BUSINESS LIKE SPORTS BUSINESS" SWEEPSTAKES

To enter, complete this entry form and mail it to be postmarked by 3/31/04 and received by 4/7/04 to:
"There's No Business Like Sports Business" Sweepstakes, PMI Station, P.O. Box 3519, Southbury, CT 06488-3519.
Limit one entry per person.

NO PURCHASE NECESSARY TO ENTER OR WIN. Open to legal residents of the 48 contiguous United States and District of Columbia,
18 or older. Void where prohibited. Subject to Official Rules on reverse.

NO PURCHASE NECESSARY TO ENTER OR CLAIM PRIZE. OFFERED ONLY IN THE 48 CONTIGUOUS UNITED STATES AND DISTRICT OF COLUMBIA ("U.S.") AND OPEN ONLY TO LEGAL U.S. RESIDENTS WHO ARE 18 YEARS OF AGE OR OLDER.

1. ELIGIBILITY: NO PURCHASE NECESSARY TO ENTER OR WIN. Open to legal residents of the 48 contiguous United States and District of Columbia who are 18 years of age or older at time of entry. Employees of Entrepreneur Press (the "Sponsor"), Steiner Sports, their respective subsidiaries, agencies, affiliates and members of the immediate families (spouses and parents, siblings, children and their spouses and in-laws) and persons living in the same household of such individuals are not eligible. Void where prohibited.

2 TO ENTER: Complete an official entry form found inside specially marked copies of "The Business Playbook: Leadership Lessons from the World of Sports" by Brandon Steiner and at in-store sweepstakes displays. Or, hand print your name, complete address, daytime and evening telephone numbers, date of birth, and email address (optional) on a 3"x5" piece of paper. Mail your entry to be postmarked by 3/31/04 and received by 4/7/04 to: "There's No Business Like Sports Business" Sweepstakes, PMI Station, P.O. Box 3519, Southbury, CT 06488-3519. Limit one entry per person.

3. PRIZE: On or about 4/15/04, a random drawing will be conducted by Promotion Mechanics, Inc., an independent judging organization, from amongall eligible entries received to award the following prize: (1) Grand Prize: two tickets to a professional sports game of the sport of winner's choice (from a list provided by Sponsor) and the opportunity to meet a Hall-of-Famer (to be determined by Sponsor) prior to the game. Prize consists of round trip transportation, two tickets to the game, and one nights' double-occupancy hotel accommodations (if winner resides more than 60 miles away from sporting event venue). All expenses not specified are winner's responsibility. Approximate retail value up to $450, however, actual value will be determined by winner's residence, sport selection and seasonal rates. Travel, accommodations, game tickets and Hall-of-Famer meeting are subject to availability and certain restrictions. In the event winner is unable to attend a game coinciding with the Hall-of-Famer visit, the Hall-of-Famer portion of the prize will be forfeited. Prize must be used by 12/30/04 or prize will be forfeited.

Winner will be notified by mail. Odds of winning will be determined by the number of eligible entries received, which is estimated to be 100,000.

4. GENERAL: By participating, entrants agree (a) to these rules and decisions of judges which shall be final in all respects; (b) to release Sponsor, Steiner Sports, and their respective parents, subsidiaries and affiliated companies, including Promotion Mechanics, Inc., and their respective directors, officers, employees, agents and representatives from any and all liability, losses or damages of any kind resulting from their participating in the promotion or their acceptance, use or misuse of a prize, including liability for personal injury or death; and (c) if a winner, to the use of name and/or photograph for advertising and publicity purposes without compensation (unless prohibited by law) and to execute specific consent to such use if asked to do so. Winner will be required to complete a declaration of eligibility and liability release and (where legal) a publicity release, which must be returned within 7 days of attempted notification or an alternate winner may be selected. Return of any prize/prize notification as undeliverable may result in disqualification of winner and selection of an alternate winner. If a winner is not of the age of majority in his/her state of residence (a "minor"), prize will be awarded in the name of a parent or legal guardian, and the release (if applicable) must also be signed by that minor's parent or legal guardian. Sponsor, its officers, directors, affiliates, subsidiaries, agents and representatives and their respective employees are not responsible and shall not be liable for late, lost, illegible, postage-due, incomplete, damaged or misdirected entries or mail; and any condition caused by events that may cause the promotion to be disrupted or corrupted. Sponsor reserves the right in its sole discretion to cancel or suspend the sweepstakes or any portion thereof should any causes beyond the control of Sponsor corrupt the administration, security or proper play of the promotion; in which case, all prizes will be awarded via a random drawing from among all eligible entries legitimately received prior to cancellation. Entries become the property of Sponsor. No prize transfer. No prize substitution except at Sponsor's sole discretion.

5. WINNERS LIST: For winner's name, mail a self-addressed, stamped envelope to be received by 4/15/04 to: "There's No Business Like Sports Business" Winner, PMI Station, PO Box 750, Southbury, CT 06488-0750. Sponsor: Entrepreneur Press, 2445 McCabe Way, Suite 400, Irvine, CA 92614. Administrator: Promotion Mechanics, Inc., 87 South Main Street, Newtown, CT 06470.

PLACE
STAMP
HERE

"There's No Business Like Sports Business" Sweepstakes
PMI Station
P.O. Box 3519
Southbury, CT 06488-3519

fight was canceled. I lost everything I had put into it. I didn't have a lot of money at the time. My staff was very small, just me and two other people, one of whom was part-time. Things were tight.

When we took that hit, I had to think about closing up shop. It was a big loss. There was very little other money coming in, and my wife, Mara, and I were thinking of starting a family. That night we had one of those face-the-music discussions. She said, "You've been at this for a while now, and maybe it's time to use your talents working for someone else's company."

I answered, "You're absolutely right. I'm with you 100 percent! I'll make some calls tomorrow and see what's out there." I went into the office the next day and decided that there was no way I was going to close down. I never made one call asking about a job. I couldn't do it! I believed too strongly in what I was doing, and when you believe that way, quitting can't be part of the plan.

I made two calls that week and went into debt for the first time. One call was to set up some direct mail advertising and the other was to hire a public relations agent. I called the biggest name in New York, Howard Rubenstein.

You see, even though there was no way I could logically afford the best, I believe that when you want to get things done, you've got to go to the best. If you want to deal with a specific company, go to the top person in the company. Decision makers can give you one of three answers, and two of them are good. They can say yes, they can refer you to someone else (and a referral from the top man is a good referral!), or they can say no.

Figuring my odds were two out of three, I gave Howard Rubenstein a call. Howard's fee at that time was about $5,000–$10,000 a month for a company the size of Steiner Sports. I said, "$5,000 isn't even close to possible. I need to be about $1,200." Because he liked me, he offered to take me on for $2,500 as a favor. I was desperate, but I couldn't do it. I said, "I understand, but I can't possibly afford more than $1,200 a month." I don't know if it was his innate goodness or my determination, or both, but he said, "I've got a good feeling about you, Brandon. I'll take you on for $1,200 a month at first." I was amazed, but I wasn't finished. I said, "Not only do I need to do this for $1,200, but I need to have a meeting with you at least once every other month." Again, he said yes! He got me earning. He took care of me personally. He's the man who gave me the break and made me a name in the business. Richard Boch, who was my personal account representative, was also very instrumental in making this relationship work.

The key to overcoming adversity is more often than not a matter of hanging in and not giving up. If you know you're doing the right thing, don't quit.

ADAPTING GOALS TO REALITY

Bill Walton earned two NBA championships and many individual honors during his playing career. Now he's gained fame as a basketball broadcaster. But his path was not a smooth one and he had to settle for the cards that fate dealt him. In a pained voice he told me:

> The injuries destroyed my career. All I ever wanted in life was more. All I ever wanted from basketball was to be able to play more. I missed the equivalent of nine full seasons in a 14-year career due to an endless series of stress fractures. My dream in life was to play against Kareem Abdul-Jabbar in the NBA finals, but I didn't get to do it.

Walton did do battle with Jabbar in the semi-finals in 1977, when the Portland Trailblazers swept Los Angeles on the way to their first and only title. To Walton, however, that's not the same thing.

But the main lesson I get from Bill was how he adapted to reality. Enduring 30 operations on his feet, he knew he would sit out hundreds of games without even removing his warm-ups. He actually missed 680 games over 14 NBA seasons. As painful as that was for him, he adopted what I call an "open-ended" plan. "I wanted to play as much basketball as I could, as best as I could," Bill told me.

His talent as a young player was off the charts. His versatility metric, if you want to call it that, was just incredible. He could leap, shoot, pass, rebound—he was the whole package. The writers who voted Bill into the Hall of Fame knew that. They gave him recognition not for what he failed to accomplish but for what he did accomplish and what more he *would* have accomplished had he stayed healthy. With so many injuries, he just had to play the cards he was dealt and wait for his opportunity.

Walton and Earl Monroe understood that success involves planning. Most of us know that. But they also knew that success could be achieved in resetting their previous goals and arriving at new plans to achieve those goals. It didn't hurt them either: Both were selected as top-50 all-time players and voted onto the NBA's 50th anniversary team in 1996.

I asked Lou Piniella, the manager of the Tampa Bay Devil Rays, how he would set goals for the 2003 season. The Devil Rays' entire team payroll is less than $20 million a year, less than the $25 million that Texas superstar Alex Rodriguez makes by himself. What realistic goals can Piniella set for his team? Tampa Bay can't compete with Eastern Division rivals like the New

An intense player in his time, Lou Piniella is one of the most intense managers in the game. Managing the Tampa Bay Devil Rays may be one of his biggest challenges.

Photo courtesy: Getty Images.

York Yankees, who spend eight times more on payroll. "I told my players we should strive to play .500 baseball," Piniella said. "There is a lot to be said if we can achieve that this year. We need to find out who wants to win and who can help us win." Piniella and his team see this season as a test and are motivated to see how far they can go. As the Yankees began their season with 11 wins and two losses, Tampa Bay could be proud that they pinned both those losses on New York.

Several years ago Steiner Sports faced an event that tested our mettle. In May 1998 David Wells pitched a perfect game for the New York Yankees, which is a sports marketer's daydream. The situation was a double winner, since it was the year that the Yankees went on to win 114 games, setting an American League record. When something is that right, even casual memorabilia collectors and fans want a memento. My partner, Jared, figured we should arrange for many of the Yankees to sign

Photo courtesy: Getty Images.

a picture of the team mobbing Wells on the mound after the last out and carrying him off the field. We figured to get a double hit, because if the team won the World Series (which it eventually did), we could go back to those same players we built relationships with during the signing and work with them in October and right through the off-season. It was a natural.

However, after a strong play, we didn't get Wells for a signing

David Wells hurls for the New York Yankees. In 1998 he pitched a perfect game.

exclusive. We thought we had a commitment, but at the last minute, he wanted more money. He had agreed to $30 for each signed piece. But Bernie Williams, who had been a Yankee since 1991, long before Wells, wanted $40 an item. So then Wells wanted $50. Jeter was getting $75 a piece, so he couldn't get that. But we had 20 Yankees signing 1,000 photos each, so we had to keep our costs down.

The way it works is you pay all the players. If a guy signs 1,000 pieces for $20 a piece, he walks out with a $20,000 check and that's it. If you don't sell those 1,000 pieces, that's your problem.

In August 1998, three months after the perfect game, we were hemorrhaging cash flow every day—paying all the other players but still without Wells.

We had a huge commitment of money for this piece, close to $500,000. It was nerve-wracking; I got a second mortgage on my home to help pay for it. In 1998 we were only a $10 million company without a parent company to back us. We didn't know what to do until Jared came up with an idea.

He suggested making a collage. We had some balls Wells had signed from a previous deal, and we mounted a close-up picture of an autographed ball at the bottom of the 16-by-20 photo. The collage also included a scorecard of the game and a brass nameplate with details of his perfect game. We added all this to the picture of the Yankees carrying Wells off the field against a pinstriped background. We were able to set

The David Wells "shadow box" sold by Steiner Sports.

Photo courtesy: Steiner Sports.

the price at about $1,500 and sold approximately 1,000 pieces and made about $1.1 million. That was one huge turning point for us, and typifies the way that Jared's creative redesign of our original plan led to success.

NEVER STOP TRYING

John Starks knows what I mean. Basketball fans in the late 1980s and early 1990s saw the early part of his career with the Golden State Warriors and New York Knicks, and 12 years later he was still at it with the Utah Jazz. But John was cut from the Golden State Warriors after his first season, got cut from the Continental Basketball Association, and was bagging groceries for a living. That's humbling. But he never stopped trying, never stopped working on his game. John got back into the CBA, then the Knicks picked him up, and he became the kind of

player New York loved—one who played with heart and energy all the time, even if he did get overly emotional at times. He went from packing groceries to a 13-year NBA career in which he reached $4 or $5 million a year—all because he never gave up. And one of the great things about John is that he doesn't just accept the good things in

John Stark's dunk over Michael Jordan.

Photo courtesy: Getty Images.

his life as his due. He gives back. He invests in the community through various charities as well as the John Starks Foundation.

Dwight Gooden is well known for overcoming his share of adversity. He went from the top of the mound, to the bottom of his drug problem, then back to the top—throwing a no-hitter in 1996. Now he works for the New York Yankees.

Successful people always find ways to turn their stumbling blocks into stepping-stones.

Rick Barry is the only player to lead both the NBA and the old ABA in scoring and was a five-time All-NBA First Team player. Barry says, "A true professional doesn't just say, 'I had a bad day, I'll get it back tomorrow,' he analyzes what went wrong and figures out how to make it better."

Believe me, if you want to find people who have overcome adversity, just find anyone who's successful. Overcoming adversity is a natural part of the journey. It may not be pleasant, but it makes you stronger and better.

—— *Chapter Review* ——

▶ Stay positive. When something negative happens, ask yourself what lesson can be learned.

▶ Turn your stumbling blocks into stepping-stones.

▶ See the opportunity in the adversity.

▶ Adversity is part of the road. Accept it and keep going.

USA's Earvin "Magic" Johnson rejoices with his gold medal after beating Croatia in the Summer Olympic basketball in Barcelona Saturday, August 8, 1992. The USA beat Croatia 117 to 85 to win the gold.

The dictionary is the only place where success comes before work.

—Anonymous.

SEE SUCCESS
AS A HABIT

S ome people are afraid of success. They feel they've never succeeded
and thus have nothing to build on as they face new challenges.
They may be mindful of a recent failure they can't forget and
become too paralyzed to go forward. Despite their failures and the negative thoughts that occupy their minds, these people have also had successes. They're just not seeing them.

We've all had them. Some people enjoy success early in life. Others
succeed later. Most of us have experienced what it's like to ace the
course, win the game, earn the degree, meet a deadline, make the sale,
get the job, help a friend in need. How did we do those things? Did success come to us willy nilly? Did we stumble onto our successes, the way
we would come across $5 while out strolling? Some successes occur that
way, but most don't. Ultimately, our successes follow considerable
efforts. We are rewarded, sometimes in wonderful and surprising ways,

for staying the course. When we make longer, more-sustained efforts, we achieve larger, more-significant goals.

The point here is that those of us who have succeeded at some task or another know we can always look back at that success and replay it in our minds—like we were cueing up a favorite song. "Aha," we say to ourselves, "that's how I did it." At that point, we feel ready to meet a new challenge.

If you've ever gone through a similar experience, you've learned the truth that success breeds success. In this way, success can become a habit. There's a revealing phrase in athletics called "muscle memory." What does it mean? Muscle memory is at work when an athlete plies her craft, her mind and body in sync, recalling how she swung the bat, shot the free throw, or kicked the ball. Muscle memory—it's an image of a body, working with a mind, recalling how it has succeeded in the past.

When athletes fall into slumps, they seem not to trust their muscle memory. They tinker. They make adjustments. "A slump," Phil Rizzuto once said, "starts in your head and ends up in your gut." You end up distrusting the very ways and instincts that helped you to succeed in the first place. To get out of that slump, an athlete has to go back to what worked. It's the same for us: Even when we've suffered a considerable failure on a project, we can direct our attention to a time when we succeeded and use what we learned then to meet a challenge, even if the challenge is a brand new one that we've never faced.

GET ADDICTED TO SUCCESS

Then, after your success, after you have reached a goal, you need to reset. Find a new challenge. No matter how good your hand might be looking, it's never too early to take the cards back and reshuffle them. Even when our initial efforts are thwarted, we've got to set new goals, with new plans based on the same simple principles. New ideas keep the world spinning.

I've asked tennis star John McEnroe, "What were you thinking of when you won your third Wimbledon title?" John told me that immediately after he won, he was thinking of how to get a fourth one. Success is addictive, and when you get some of it, you want to get more. Michael Jordan won his first NBA title with Chicago in 1991. But he was driven by the thought that people might regard him and his teammates as flukes if they won only one. Chicago won successive titles in the following two years and then three more after Jordan came out of retirement. Bill Parcells, John McEnroe, Derek Jeter, Pat Riley—every winner tells me the same thing, they want that taste again and again. It's the same with tens of millions of winners in business.

But the discipline is key. People sometimes forget this point. Notice how often we observe a great athlete and think their skills are innate. It's revealed in the way people talk about athletes. So Ted Williams hitting a baseball was "a natural." Michael Jordan is "gifted." Sure, these people have natural endowments. They couldn't compete at a championship level without a very high talent quotient. But they possess more than talent. I like to look at how athletes face challenges, overcome them, and then face new ones all over again, as if the old ones were already behind them.

The work ethic was always apparent with Michael Jordan, too. Anyone who holds the opinion that Air Jordan just flew through his career without an effort should examine Jordan's repeated challenges and the way he overcame them. As he enters his last retirement, he'll have another challenge, maybe his largest: finding something new to compete at.

Anyone who is great in athletics has had to hone their craft. They have to spend time analyzing defeats, recalling past successes, and working to find new ways to succeed. Pat Riley might be the first to tell you that he had little natural ability as a player. Still, he played on the Los Angeles Lakers 1972 team that won 69 games, a record at the time, and set a record that may never be broken—33 wins in a row. The average

KEEP YOUR EYE ON THE BALL

To borrow the sports vernacular of our time, Ted Williams was focused, utterly focused, on hitting a ball. His success was as many parts discipline as it was talent. So Williams refined the *The Science of Hitting*—his book by that name still rates as a classic and has been read by recent greats such as Tony Gwynn, Wade Boggs, and other great batsmen. The 6-foot-4-inch, 195-pound "Splendid Splinter," a name given to him by Mel Allen, the late Yankee broadcaster, was simply the shrewdest hitter ever to grip a bat. So astute was Williams' hitting that he mentally divided the 16-inch width of home plate and the strike zone from knees to shoulders into a grid of imaginary boxes. A box inside and high was a .390 sweet spot; outside and low, a .230 abyss. At the root of this grid of 77 little boxes, each with its own batting average, was Williams' conviction that the first rule of hitting was to find a good pitch to hit.

Williams' crowning glory was his 1941 season, when he closed the year with six hits in eight at bats in a doubleheader to bat .406. Before he got a chance to follow up his miraculous campaign, the 23-year-old enlisted in the Navy Air Corps in May 1942, spending three and a half seasons in the military, primarily training other pilots. He later returned as a Marine pilot in Korea. In sum, Williams missed all or part of five seasons to military service, yet still posted excellent seasons after returning to the Red Sox lineup in August 1953. Williams said what he wanted out of life was to walk down the street and have someone say, "There goes the best hitter that ever lived." That was his goal, and many people say he achieved it.

What I want to point out is the human aspect of Williams' achievement. He suffered many interruptions to his goal but he just kept on going. Do you think talent carried him through when he returned home from Korea, at 34, with his youth already behind him? I doubt it. His goal to be the best drove him on and on. He wasn't a machine; he fought through periods where he lost his stroke and had to find it and refine it all over again. Still, he managed to achieve his goal of being the greatest hitter—certainly the greatest hitter of his time—and also found time to be an American hero, too. John Glenn, who served with Williams in Korea and later became his friend, said "Ted Williams is the greatest I've seen at three things: fly fishing, hitting a baseball, and being a wing pilot."

Photo courtesy: Getty Images.

NBA career is still only four years, but Riley had the drive to stay around for nine years. When he made a public speaking appearance for Steiner Sports, I saw in his unusually diligent preparation the same relentless drive that must have carried him through those playing days.

PURSUE SUCCESS IN MANY AREAS OF LIFE

Some of the greatest successes emerge against a backdrop of challenges, even losses. Bobby Valentine was recently fired as manager of the New

York Mets. But turning challenges into success was already a habit with Bobby long before that happened. He has faced serious obstacles in his career since he was 20.

One of my injuries was probably my first obstacle. I got beaned in 1970. I was 20 years old so everything was pretty smooth until then. I had a lot of success. I led the Pacific Coast League in hitting (and was selected Player of the Year). A guy named Greg Washburn threw the pitch; it fractured my cheekbone. It was the last day of the season. But I was having a good season, an MVP season. I was playing AAA ball and, I was supposed to get to the big leagues the next year. So there were a couple of weeks in the hospital with my head in bandages, figuring out if I was going to play again. It didn't turn out to be an obstacle because two months later, I was playing winter ball.

Adversity struck harder three years later. He was playing for the California Angels in 1973 when he ran into a wall while chasing a fly ball. Valentine had made his mark as a speedster, but the collision wrecked his leg, breaking it in two places. "I was thinking, 'Just shoot me,'" he recalled. His speed had been a large part of his game. Now he had to learn to play several different positions. "I had to play left field and third base, places where I couldn't run, where my speed wasn't a factor, as my knee was getting better. I wore one of those big Joe Namath knee braces."

In 1974 he separated his shoulder. After ten injury-ridden seasons with five clubs, he called it quits in 1979. He didn't enjoy a single season uninterrupted by debilitating injuries. Five years later, he became a manager with the Texas Rangers. He had become the Mets' manager by 1996, and in 2000, took them to the World Series, where they lost to the Yankees.

Did the Mets fail the following two years because of their manager? As a manager of people, you can only ride as far as your horses will go. The Mets had one of the largest payrolls in baseball, paying 25 players more than $100 million. But the performance of many players fell short. Some players were overweight and out of shape. Others seemed to play without discipline, even giving high fives to members of the opposite team—on the field, during losses! That kind of behavior does reflect on the manager. There are two teams in New York, and no one can recall the last time anyone on the Yankees acted in similar fashion. No Mets player emerged as a leader on the field. So who was failing? The saying goes that you can't fire the players, so you fire the manager.

But if Valentine did fail on the field, he was succeeding in other areas of his life at the same time. The Mets were playing on the road on September 11, 2001, when America was attacked. What he saw and felt at that time led him to get very involved in relief efforts.

My thinking there was that I just believed there were things that had to get done and I felt caged in for a day or two watching CNN. It was totally overwhelming. I was in Pittsburgh and just saw it on TV. And then the other Pennsylvania plane came down about 50 miles from where we were. We drove home by bus on the Jersey side and drove across the bridge. Manhattan was different. There was no skyline that day. It was smoke-covered. We got home and got down to Ground Zero about two days later. I was with some of the rescue guys and it was different. I love New York City and in particular I love the skyline. It was like nothing I hope I ever see again. Did that motivate me? I don't know. Did I motivate people? I don't know. But I thought that there were things to do and I wanted to do them. I don't know what the hell I was all about. So I wanted to get out. I wanted to do something. And right from that second day on I felt that the more visible we could be—being active, being happy, being caring and sharing— then the easier it's going to be for other people. If I wasn't doing that, then how could I expect anyone else to get back to any kind of normalcy? I still believe that. I think that there's still a lot of time that needs to be given to people. There's a lot of attention, caring, and I think we got away from that a little before September 11. I think people were really going on their own ways a lot, and I think since then people have banded together a little more to make things happen collectively, rather than individually, which is a good thing. I like that.

Valentine worked around the clock to lend a hand in a dire situation. He and Mets players visited the workers who were searching for survivors at the World Trade Center site. He thought that his presence

and that of the players might contribute in a small way to keeping up morale at the site. Shea Stadium's expansive parking lot was used as a relay point from which food, water, and supplies were shipped.

Early in 2003, Valentine and the Mets were recognized by the Patrolmen's Benevolent Association, the Sergeants' Benevolent Association, and the Detectives' Endowment Association of New

Bobby Valentine was instrumental in aiding the volunteers after the September 11th disaster.

Photo courtesy: Getty Images.

York City for their post-September 11 contributions. The banquet included Police Commissioner Raymond Kelly and families of victims of the terrorist attacks.

"The real spirit was Bobby V. He basically motivated the players. And I think those players will be grateful for a long time. He pointed out they had a greater responsibility," said Deputy Chief Ed Cannon.

"I'm trying to do a lot of things," Valentine said. "I have more time now—which is the good news and the bad news. The good news is people know that I give, so I'm out there receiving—because when you give, you receive. I'm having a good time doing it.

"The president said, 'We will never forget.' I've become a little amazed at how many people didn't hear that. And what I found is the old adage of time healing all wounds is not a truism. You need many other ingredients during that time to heal the wounds." Valentine is a living example of someone who saw a purpose larger than his own amid the baseball season of 2001. Even while his team was playing a disappointing brand of ball, he was succeeding at a more lasting, more important task. Can there be any doubt that someone who has faced as many challenges as he has, and has succeeded so often, will succeed again in future endeavors?

If you're not sure what areas of your life are really most important to you, try this. Imagine your own funeral. What would you like people to be saying about you? Your spouse, family, friends, clergyman, associates—what would you want them to say? Would they say those things about you right now? If not, then you can see which areas of your life need work.

CHECKLIST FOR CHAMPIONS

How can you do it? I hope I've provided a kind of checklist for champions. Here is a list of principles that, if followed, greatly increase the chance of a successful life of action.

Remember, we all set goals, but realistic goals must (1) be specific, (2) have a date for completion, and (3) realistically achievable. Crucial to the idea of achieving goals is having a map to getting there and measuring the progress. There are measurements in sports, in business, but at times we must be honest enough to measure our own progress, even when no one else is.

Maps are one thing, but to attain our goals, it helps to find our niche. Most successful people I know have a style and a path that is their own. Their message for us is simple: We can't busy ourselves emulating what others have done. It works better to find something few people, or better yet no one, have undertaken. You don't find successful business people having the precise objectives that others have.

Once we've carved out an area to excel in, we have to energize ourselves. "Wake up nervous" means you start the day with that edge and keep on keeping on. A little nervousness, a little fear of failure, can actually drive us to succeed. There is simply no substitute for pursuing your objectives with energy. Without passion for what you do, you can't pull it off.

We need to go after our goals with abandon. But goals are about personal objectives only. Purposes involve and deal with the goals of others, not just our own. To succeed, we must ultimately think about the desires of others, of how to meet their needs, and how to work with a team when that's required. Even the greatest athletes—Gretzky, Jordan, Payton, others—come to understand they can't go it alone in team sports. Their own purposes are best served while involving others. There is no "I" in team.

In every endeavor, the very best results are attained by those willing to go the extra mile. There are athletes who have succeeded more with the size of their hearts than with extra muscle. They do what it takes, giving more of themselves, when that extra is needed. Putting in extra time at their craft, they manage their day better and increase their capacity for work.

Even when the trail seems dimly lit, staying on it can bring a good end. You never know. Effort spent on achieving the most difficult tasks, even tasks previously failed, is rewarded.

When people don't find quick success at a task, they can grow frustrated. All the negativity that accompanies setbacks seems to pile on. But focusing on what is positive—on what can be done to put yourself in a better situation to succeed—is often all that is needed. It may be more preparation, more knowledge of what the task requires—every job has its special demands and if you don't conform to what those demands are, then you reduce your chances of succeeding.

After achieving a success, some people are afraid to roll the dice and try another path. I know many people who have gotten "comfortable" doing the same darned thing for years, decades, even their whole lives. If it makes them happy, then there's not much wrong with that. The problem is, it often doesn't make them happy. They're secure, staid, contented, stale. They may appear to others to be happy and successful, but to themselves they aren't. They don't want to risk a change for fear of losing a way of doing things that works for them. But there's another problem: Without significant change, there can be no growth. Without dynamic dissatisfaction, we would all stay the paths we're on. In the aggregate, there would have been no bridges, no cars, no skyscrapers, simply put, nothing new and better. "If it ain't broke, don't fix it" is a recipe for being stuck in the mud; it is not a recipe for champions.

I haven't talked to a successful person yet who hasn't suffered his share of adversity. It's not just what happens to us in our lives, it's what we do with what happens. If you have your health, you have what you need to persevere. People in all times and all places have overcome poor upbringings, split homes, bad deals, blowout injuries, painful divorces, things they have great difficulty putting behind them. We never quite put those things behind us. But we can motivate ourselves to push on because of, even in spite of, our setbacks.

When you have success in one area, that success can help motivate you in another area. The challenge comes when, after great success, the next thing or two or three that you attempt may not "hit." That doesn't mean that great success can't or won't happen again, it just means you need to keep going.

We all have that ability to keep pressing on. It's in you and in me. Life is only really a rich experience when we drive toward a goal and know how to get there.

—— *Chapter Review* ——

▸ Success builds on success. When you reach a goal, reshuffle the cards and seek out new objectives.

▸ Success in one area helps lead to success in other areas. Build the habit by reviewing your successes.

SUGGESTED READING

Covey, Stephen. *The 7 Habits of Highly Effective People: Powerful Lessons in Personal Change.* New York: Simon and Schuster, 1989.

Riley, Pat. *The Winner Within: A Life Plan for Team Players.* New York: G.P. Putnam's, 1993.

Torre, Joe. *12 Keys for Managing Team Players, Tough Bosses, Setbacks, and Success.* New York: Hyperion, 1999

Walton, Bill. *Nothing But Net: Just Give me the Ball and Get out of the Way.* New York: Hyperion, 1994.

Wooden, John. *Wooden: A Lifetime of Observations and Reflections On and Off the Court.* Chicago: Contemporary Books, 1997.

STEINERISMS

It's not the game, it's the game plan.

If it isn't easy, it isn't possible—simplify the things you do everyday so you have more free time and less aggravation.

Don't buy any food at a sporting event till after the 1st inning or 1st quarter (it could be left over from the game before).

Don't eat seafood at a restaurant on a Sunday—it was probably at best ordered and received on Friday, so it's at least two days old.

If you're going on an airplane for a business trip—pack some healthful food and snacks so when you arrive you are 100 percent. Don't eat airplane food or airport food!

If you're going to make a recommendation to someone to buy something —do it from the heart not just the most expensive thing or item you're making the most money on.

If you're going to argue or fight for something—make sure you know what you want to win.

Take the time to get honest feedback from the people you trust so you can really see how you are good, bad, and ugly. The earlier you do this the better and the easier!

Always count your change—in the world of computers and calculators—no one can count any more and most times your change is wrong. Check it out.

If you put out good—you will get back good—put out bad and you get back bad.

Most of us are not ready for something great to happen. You only need to make one great sale in your life and sometimes it's staring you right in the face. Are you ready for it to happen? I mean *really* ready?

If you're going to do business with someone—why not ask for business back. Tell everyone around you what you do—does your drycleaner know what you do? Your gardener, the bartender, or the server at your favorite tavern know what you are trying to sell? Does your entire family know? (They are your biggest fans!)

Don't buy any drinks that dispense from clear fountain—that serves grape drink or any of those noncarbonated drinks. Those machines are full of bacteria and are very hard to clean.

When asking for a raise at work—make sure you know what else you can do to earn it. Make sure the time is right; make sure you give your employer time to respond; make sure you ask for more responsibility/ work to go with more pay and show how you can help make the company more money. Never give ultimatums unless your really mean it, and even then there is no reason to. Oh yeah, don't take advice about raises from your parents.

Capacity is all a state of mind. (Trust me, you're not close to your capacity.)

When some one tells you no—it means that they probably don't know so instead of pushing for yes—get them to know!

To be able to negotiate the best deal takes patience—usually the longer you can wait gives you the advantage to getting a smarter and sometimes better deal—as former UCLA coach John Wooden says, be quick but don't rush!

You can always find 10 to 20 percent more then you think. Growing your business is a little like stretching your hamstrings. There is a fine line between comfort and discomfort.

—Anthony Isola, personal trainer

If you can't change the people around you, change the people around you.

—Chuck D.

Be like a turtle—hard on outside, soft on the inside, and willing to stick your neck out.

—Gordie Howe

It's not who you know. It's not what you know. It's what you know about who.

—Jeffrey Berman

If you're not making some mistakes, you're probably not helping your team.

—Larry Brown, coach of NBA '76ers

People respect what you inspect—you gotta follow up all the time with everyone.

—Mitch Modell

In order to clean up a mess, sometimes more of a mess has to be made.

—Mr. Richard, founder of PC Richards Appliance Stores

If you use your head you won't have to use your feet.

—My grandmother

What type of employee are you? Are you f.a.t.???—faithful, available, and teachable?

—Pat Riley coach of the Miami Heat

About the Author

Brandon Steiner is the founder and chairman of Steiner Sports Marketing in New Rochelle, New York. The business is firmly entrenched as a leader in the marketing and collectibles industry. Once a one-man shop, Steiner Sports has grown into an 80-employee, $35 million enterprise, specializing in connecting athletes with corporate America through innovative programs. The company also offers a wide variety of high-profile, authentic memorabilia items on www.steinersports.com from a veritable who's who in the world of sports.

His roster boasts more than 500 male and female professional athletes, superstars of today and yesteryear from virtually every sport, including: the New York Yankees manager Joe Torre; All-Star shortstop Derek Jeter; six-time Wimbledon champion Billy Jean King; newly inducted baseball Hall of Famers Carlton Fisk, Dave Winfield, Gary Carter, Eddie Murray, and Ozzie Smith; women's soccer star Mia Hamm; and "Famous Moments" heroes Phil Rizzuto, Walt Frazier, Franco Harris, Marano Rivera, Mookie Wilson, Bill Buckner, and many others.

Steiner grew up in Brooklyn and was exposed to poverty in a Flatbush neighborhood. From his mother (his parents were divorced) he learned the importance of hard work and developing a reputation for being reliable and amiable. At age 5 he had a lemonade stand; at 10, a fruit delivery service. The next year he got a paper route. In his early teens he developed his own business, delivering bagels and milk to old and house-bound people. By being on time and friendly he became, in his words, "an entity in the neighborhood."

Photo courtesy: Steiner Sports.

Brandon Steiner in action!

He graduated with a business degree from Syracuse University, and joined the management training program at Hyatt Hotels. He excelled, receiving three promotions in two years. "That was the corporate experience I needed," says Steiner. "I became a well-rounded businessman and learned how corporate America makes money." From there he was offered an assistant general manager's job at the Hard Rock Cafe, where he began meeting athletes.

While opening a series of New York City sports bars he met more athletes, including many 1980s stars of the New York Mets, such as Keith Hernandez, Ron Darling, and Darryl Strawberry, and other New York sports legends such as Joe Morris and Lawrence Taylor from the Giants. Friendships developed and Steiner knew the kinds of situations they would flourish in. Some would give incentive talks for corporations; others would sign autographs or appear at franchise openings.

Three turning points took Steiner Sports to another level. One was the signing of New York Yankee great Phil Rizzuto to a lifetime marketing contract upon his entry into the Hall of Fame in 1994. Another was the exclusive signing of New York Ranger captain Mark Messier when the Rangers won the Stanley Cup in 1994. Then in 1999 Derek Jeter signed an exclusive with Steiner.

Steiner Sports now arranges more than 2,000 celebrity appearances a year. "Our in-depth relationships in the marketplace are second to none," Steiner says. "There's not a better company to call to get sports celebrity talent. Our creativity stands alone."

Steiner's impact on the sports world was recognized by *The New York Daily News* in their list of the most 40 influential people in New York, and by *GQ* as one of the up and coming sports marketing companies. He appears regularly on CNBC's *Squawk Box*, CNN's *Money Line*, and co-hosts *What's It Worth?* a collectibles program on the Yankees' YES Network. He also contributes to the Metro Bid New York Auction Show.

Brandon Steiner resides in Westchester, New York with his wife, Mara, and two children.

The Steiner Sports Web site is www.steinersports.com. He can be reached personally at brandon_s@steinersports.com or (800) 759-7267.

THE FINISHED PRODUCT

An author of several of his own books, Kenneth Shouler proposed this book and found a home for it at Entrepreneur Press. He interviewed many athletes, and wrote the text for this book.

Ken Shouler runs Wordsworth Writing and Editing in Harrison, New York. He has authored three books—two on baseball and one on basketball—and ghostwritten three others, including a forthcoming book on militant Islam.

He was chosen by Major League Baseball as one of the panelists to choose baseball's "All-Century Team" and has appeared on Fox, NBC, and the History Channel. He is a regular contributor to *Cigar Aficionado* magazine and teaches philosophy in the City University of New York.

IN THE EARLY YEARS

Cary Steiner was instrumental in arranging my early ideas for a manuscript into chapters. Here is his story.

Cary Steiner, 48, is a freelance writer and computer software trainer. He has written training manuals for a major insurance company on such topics as prospecting, telephone techniques, customer service, and positive assertiveness. He wrote and narrated a new product introduction for a Bayer Company annual sales meeting and has written user reference manuals for several kinds of software. He has edited copy for computer textbooks used by schoolchildren in India. He has also been a regular contributor to the Dat@base column in *The Rotarian* magazine. Cary is currently working on a new retelling of the Hindu epic, The Ramayana.

As an independent software training consultant, Cary has done training for the U.S. Government, Productivity Point International, Fidelity Investments, and many other corporations. He has been an instructor in adult education and special programs in the Garden City

School District. Cary was also the founder of Actors Recovery Theatre and its artistic director from 1991 until 1996. He lives in New Hyde Park, New York with his wife, Lillian, and their two teenage daughters.

INDEX